INSIGHT POCKET GUIDE

B

GW00361983

**APA** PUBLICATIONS

Part of the Langenscheidt Publishing Group

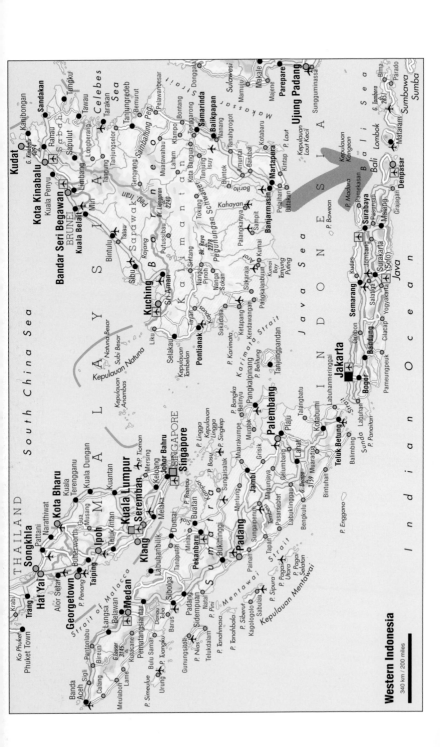

Western Indonesia

340 km / 200 miles

Welcome

This guidebook combines the interests and enthusiasms of two of the world's best-known information providers: Insight Guides, who have set the standard for visual travel guides since 1970, and Discovery Channel, the world's premier source of non-fiction television programming. Its aim is to bring you the best of Bali in a series of tailor-made itineraries devised by Insight's Bali correspondent, Garrett Kam.

Both magical and mythical, this land of volcanic lakes, spectacular rice terraces and ancient temples and palaces is a melting cauldron of cultures and peoples. Renowned for its unsurpassed traditional architecture, theatre and dance, and elaborate religious festivals, the evocative Balinese culture is a lively and dynamic force that is constantly synthesising the old and the new, the traditional with the innovative. The itineraries in this book are arranged according to the main geographical regions of Bali, each area seamlessly connecting with the other while covering all the must-see sights as well as the lesser-known attractions. You could travel the length and breadth of Bali – from coast to crater – by changing your base every few days, but if pressed for time, stay at the popular beach areas of the south or in Ubud, the cultural heartland of Bali, and choose to discover the regions that interest you most. Chapters on shopping, eating out and nightlife, plus a practical information section on travel essentials complete this reader-friendly guide.

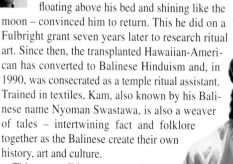

Garrett Kam first step foot on Bali in 1980 while he was studying dance in Java, but the magic of the island – including a dream encounter with an old man dressed in white, floating above his bed and shining like the moon – convinced him to return. This he did on a Fulbright grant seven years later to research ritual art. Since then, the transplanted Hawaiian-American has converted to Balinese Hinduism and, in 1990, was consecrated as a temple ritual assistant. Trained in textiles, Kam, also known by his Balinese name Nyoman Swastawa, is also a weaver of tales – intertwining fact and folklore together as the Balinese create their own history, art and culture.

This new edition was completely restructured and rewritten by Kam and owes its foundations to the original edition put together by another foreign-born Balinese resident, Made Wijaya.

Pages 2/3: rice terraces define Bali's landscape
Pages 8/9: offerings of fruit and flowers at a temple festival

History *&Culture*

'Island of the Gods', 'Island of Demons', 'Island of Temples', 'Island of Music and Dance'…. These cliched epithets of Bali are varied but all of them are true. After all, this wonderful tropical island is one of the few places in the world blessed with such extraordinary natural beauty, lovely and talented people, and a colourful culture centred on religion.

Bali has experienced many diverse influences over the centuries due to its geographic position in the middle of Indonesia, the world's largest archipelago and still an important stop in the international maritime trade route today. Indian deities and mythology, Chinese motifs in carving and textiles, music and dance forms derived from Java, and open-sided Pacific-style pavilions with thatched roofs resting on rows of pillars all have found fertile ground for fusion and growth on the tropical island.

A Tumultuous History

Historically, an independent Buddhist kingdom was already well-established on Bali by the 5th century. In the 11th century, however, Bali was absorbed by Hindu Java through the royal marriage of the island's King Udayana and the East Javanese princess Mahendradatta. Through this union, Hinduism fused with Buddhism in Bali, incorporating indigenous animistic beliefs and ancestral worship with Indian deities.

Bali, however, always managed to regain its independence whenever the political situation on Java weakened or changed, especially as Islam gained ground in the archipelago during the 15th century but spared Bali. Through centuries of warfare, various kings carved out their own territories on the island.

European colonial intrusions from the 17th century onwards made the situation even more tenuous. By the early 20th century, Dutch military campaigns – which saw thousands of Balinese nobility committing mass suicide, or *puputan*, rather than surrender – had put a violent end to the Balinese ruling houses. One of the consequences was that traditional patronage of the arts shifted from the courts to foreigners. To make it a productive part of the Netherlands Indies, Bali was promoted as a unique Hindu enclave, much to the detriment of the island's older Buddhist heritage.

The brief but tumultuous Dutch rule ended when the Japanese invaded Bali in 1942. Although the Japanese – who proved to be more despotic than the Dutch had ever been – left just three years later, it was clear that the proud Balinese would never be in foreign hands again. Nationalist organisations that had taken root in the meantime were preparing to fight the

Left: cremation ceremony
Right: Balinese warrior of the 1880s

returning Dutch. The Republic of Indonesia was officially proclaimed on 17 August 1945, but it took another four years before the Dutch officially recognised Indonesia's independence and Bali's right as a province.

In the area of the arts, however, Western influence was far more successful. During the 1920s, European artists like Walter Spies and Rudolph Bennett introduced Western aesthetics and methods to the Balinese, giving rise to different styles of painting and woodcarving that tourists purchased as souvenirs. Today, a centuries-old style of classical painting co-exists with innovative contemporary art, and thousands of villagers produce craft items both for the local tourism market as well as for export. Traditional village architects rebuild temples using time-honoured principles, while their university-trained counterparts design luxury hotels incorporating Balinese elements.

All of these activities are part of a creative process that has been going on for centuries in Bali. The resilience of Balinese culture comes from its remarkable ability to adopt, adapt and absorb. Strong indigenous traditions, coupled with receptivity to new ideas, has led to the transformation and integration of a multitude of ideas that have become the Balinese mosaic of life as seen today.

The history of Bali, since the 1960s, has been defined and propelled forward by tourism and its related commercial spin-offs. While some, like Balinese anthropologist Bangkal Kusuma, charge that it has resulted in the loss of Balinese innocence and a 'McDonaldisation' of its traditional culture and values, it is clear that tourism has been the making of Bali over the past few decades. In the island's arts and crafts industry and in the performing arts at least, there can be no doubt of tourism's revitalising effects.

Community & Society

Balinese society is highly structured, and both hierarchical and communal at the same time. The *banjar* (neighbourhood), to which every married male householder is a member with full duties and representative rights, oversees the conduct of temple matters and administers *adat* (traditional laws) that govern the community. Births, deaths, marriages, divorce, property disputes and infringements of the law are all the business of the neighbourhood association.

Above: contemporary art depicting Balinese life

history/culture

Balinese society is still quasi-feudal in that titles, customs and social protocol of the kingdom-days are still in effect. All Balinese are members of genealogical clan groups that number in the hundreds, with up to 95 percent of them belonging to the *sudra* (commoner) or *jaba* (outsider) caste.

Commoner names are prefixed first by I (pronounced 'ee') for a male or Ni for a female, then according to birth order by Wayan (Putu, Gede), Made (Kadek, Nengah), Nyoman (Komang) and Ketut; the sequence repeats if there are more than four children. A personal name follows this birth order name.

The *triwangsa* (three upper castes) are *wesia* (merchants), prefixed by I Gusti Ngurah for a man, or Ni Gusti Ayu for a woman; *kasatria* (royalty), indicated by Dalem, Cokorda, Dewa, Anak Agung, Desak, Pungakan (or Ngakan); and *brahmana* (high priests), with the title Ida Bagus for a man or Ida Ayu for a woman.

The caste system gives rise to many names and titles from which one can discern a person's lineage. Ida Bagus Ekaputra, for example, would be the first son of *brahmana* parents. Anak Agung Istri Made Rai would be a second- (or sixth-, or tenth-) born daughter with a princely father and commoner mother. All this might seem rather complicated, but social distinctions play a major role in keeping alive the theatre of Balinese life.

Status is also reinforced through the various levels of the Balinese language. Low Balinese is spoken by the higher castes to the lower ones, and among social equals, friends and family. High Balinese, derived from Javanese, is used for strangers and social superiors. There also is a Middle Balinese, varying mixtures of low and high levels for finer distinctions of expression and status. Each level has its own set of special vocabularies.

In addition to this linguistic complexity, there is Kawi, the language of priestly ritual and often used in dramas, which borrows many words from Sanskrit, the ancient language of India. Many young Balinese mix together their own tongue with the national language, Bahasa Indonesia.

Religion & Ritual

Religion is at the core of Balinese life. Known as Agama Hindu-Dharma (or Agama Tirtha, the Religion of Holy Water, because of the importance of the sacred liquid), it is concerned with *yadnya* (sacrifices) to five kinds of beings: *dewa* (deities, deified ancestors), *buta* (demons), *manusa* (humans), *pitra* (deceased) and *resi* (holy people).

Essential to every ritual are *banten* (offerings), gifts made of rice, meat, cakes, biscuits, flowers, betel nuts and palm leaf figures, along with a little donation to the temple. Offerings are first purified with a sprinkling of holy water before the essence is directed to a deity or spirit by a *pemangku* (temple priest or priestess) with incense and *mantra* (incantations).

People then pray using incense and flowers, followed by a sprinkling of holy water which they also sip and wipe over the face. Grains of raw rice soaked in water are stuck on the forehead, temples and throat, and then swallowed. Worshippers

Right: religious offerings

take the physical parts of the offerings home as *lungsuran* (leftovers) to consume as they please. Demon offerings, including blood spilled during a cockfight, are directed to the lower elemental forces and placed on the ground, then discarded after the ritual has ended.

Although the Balinese insist that their religion is monotheistic (in accordance with the Indonesian policy of *Pancasila*, which recognises the belief in one God), they usually pray to the myriad manifestations of Sanghyang Widhi Wasa, including the vast Hindu pantheon of gods, Buddha, deified ancestors and a wide range of elemental spirits. The other four basic Balinese religious principles are belief in the individual soul, that each soul is subject to *karma-pala* (present actions that bear consequences in the next life), reincarnation, and eventual release of the soul from the cycles of rebirth.

Most Balinese are very religious although they are not concerned with spirituality or mysticism. Belief in black magic and evil spirits, especially in causing illness, is being replaced by a growing faith in Western medicine. Nonetheless, genuine trance rituals still take place even in tourist centres, and practitioners of black and white magic still have faithful clients.

Religion is the focus of the Balinese creative conscience, pervading everything from the cultivation of rice terraces to elaborate temple offerings. Hardly a day passes without a colourful procession spirited on by the hypnotic music of a *gamelan*. Most of the artistry is directed towards building temples and creating figures and paintings for temples. Traditional Balinese architecture, with its airy pavilions and towering carved gates, is a harmonious fusion of buildings with their surroundings. The many rites of passage also provide occasions for the performing arts.

Dance & Theatre

Theatre is an integral part of Balinese life and is tied closely to religion, as ceremonies are times for traditional entertainment. Narrative poetry is often recited in stylised voices during a ritual, but most people ignore it and prefer to listen to the dynamic interlocking music of the *gamelan*. Instead, the traditional medium of moral instruction comes from the many forms of theatre where Hindu epics, historical legends and human problems and ideals are re-enacted. The true function of music and theatre during a religious ritual, however, is believed to be entertainment for invisible deities and spirits.

Balinese performing arts are celebrations of creative human genius, especially when allied with spiritual power. The spirit of *taksu* (supernatural charisma) enters some dancers, giving them divine inspiration and adding a magical quality to their performances. Below is a summary of the more common forms of traditional entertainment (see *page 97* for performance times and venues):

Barong & Rangda: The lion-like Barong, the force of protection and healing, confronts the chaotic and malevolent Rangda. Their battle, which ends in a temporary quelling rather than victory, often occurs within the context of the exorcist drama, *Calonarang*. It tells of a legendary Javanese queen who, out of jealousy, uses black magic to kill her Balinese

Left: a topeng dancer

husband for taking another wife. The queen, now called Rangda (widow), and her daughter are banished by her son. Due to Rangda's reputation, no one wants to marry her daughter, so she seeks revenge by causing epidemics in the kingdom. One man finally pretends to propose, steals Rangda's book of witchcraft, and gives it to his priestly father, who assumes the form of the Barong. In anger, Rangda transforms into a terrifying witch. Entranced men armed with *keris* (daggers) attempt to kill Rangda, but her power makes them try to stab themselves instead. However, the Barong prevents them from harm. White-clothed *pemangku* (temple priests) wait nearby to revive them with splashes of holy water, and harmony is restored. Performances for tourists, however, show a different tale in which a goddess, cursed into a horrific form for having offended her husband, has her beauty restored by a young hero, who is presented as a sacrifice to her.

Kecak: Choreographed during the 1930s and based on *sanghyang* (exorcist dance), this circular seated chorus of dozens of bare-chested men dressed in knee-length trousers and loincloth becomes a forest, an army of monkeys and whatever else, as principal dancers take on roles from the *Ramayana*.

Sanghyang Dedari and **Sanghyang Jaran**: In the first, two girls are brought into a state of trance through songs and chants, dancing as *dedari* (celestial maidens) in unison with their eyes shut. In the second, an entranced man dances on a *jaran* (hobby horse) barefoot among burning coconut husks.

Rejang: Slow ceremonial temple dances with repetitive movements done by girls and women. Most villages have their own styles of dance.

Gambuh: Elegant dance drama of Javanese-Balinese *Malat* or *Panji* romances. Performers speak with stylised voices in archaic Kawi, with music by long bamboo flutes, vertical fiddles, drums, gongs and a variety of bronze percussion instruments.

Arja: Romantic operetta using *Malat* stories in which dancers sing and speak their own dialogue to the accompaniment of *gamelan* music. All-male groups are very popular due to their burlesque and campy humour.

Topeng: Performed in temples by a soloist (or up to five dancers) who changes *topeng* (masks) many times to become different figures to tell legendary histories of Balinese kingdoms.

Above: *kecak* – modern dance variation on an ancient theme

Telek & Jauk: Masked dances with refined figures fluttering fans, or rough characters with long fingernails, sometimes with Barong-Rangda play.

Wayang Wong: Masked dance dramas of the *Ramayana* epic, usually performed during temple festivals. Human characters may be unmasked, and all players speak their own lines while a narrator describes scenes.

Sendratari: Created during the 1960s, *sendratari* (*seni* means 'art', *drama tari* means 'dance drama') has a narrator reciting a story as dancers mime dialogue taken from *Ramayana* and *Mahabharata* episodes.

Drama Gong: Dramatic play created with soap-opera-like stories. A *gamelan* plays music, and the dialogue is laced with ribald humour.

Joged: Social dance, with music by bamboo xylophones, in which a young woman dances alone and then selects a man from the audience by tapping him with her fan.

Janger: Appeared during the early 1900s as a children's dance, with groups of girls and boys singing folk songs and dancing simple movements in different formations; may include a narrative story.

Tari Kodok (Frog Dance): Children dressed as frogs dance to the buzzing sounds of *genggong* (jaw-harps), drums, cymbals and reed pipes as they perform the folktale of a princess who falls in love with a frog – who really is a handsome prince in disguise.

Gebyug: Groups of men dance and make their music with giant wooden cowbells, then accompany a dance drama of a hunter who finds salvation.

Tari Lepas: These programmes present a variety of dances and open with *panyembrama* performed by girls who welcome the audience by tossing flower petals, based on improvised *pendet* and *gabor* dances performed during temple rituals in honour of the deities. Other dances may include *legong*, a highly-stylised narrative court dance performed by two or three girls and *baris*, where a young boy depicts a warrior, or groups of men dance and fight with different weapons for temple ceremonies. There are also several bird and animal dances done by children, for instance the *oleg tambulilingan* where a female bee is joined by a male bee for a love duet.

Wayang Kulit: Leather puppet theatre has shadows cast by a flaming oil lamp onto a cloth screen, or visible in all their colourful details without a screen during temple ceremonies for *wayang lemah*. The *dalang* (puppeteer) has astonishing skills in handling up to 100 figures and giving each of them special voices while conducting musicians for up to four hours without taking any breaks.

HISTORY HIGHLIGHTS

2500–1500 BC Migrants from southern China and mainland Southeast Asia reach the archipelago and mix with aboriginal peoples.

300 Bronze-age culture in Bali.

AD 78 Indian civilisation begins to make an impact.

500 Chinese traders mention Buddhist kingdom of P'oli (Bali).

800 Buddhist Warmadewa dynasty rules Bali; inscriptions in Old Balinese.

1000 Airlangga, son of a Balinese king and Javanese queen, becomes king in East Java, while his younger brother, Anak Wungsu, rules Bali (1035); Javanese influence increases in Bali; during civil war in Java, Bali becomes independent (1045).

1200 Javanese Singasari kingdom retakes Bali (1284); forces of Kublai Khan attack Java, and Bali breaks free again (1292).

1300 The Javanese Hindu-Buddhist Majapahit kingdom conquers Bali (1343); Gelgel kingdom unifies Bali (1383).

1400 Islam spreads to the archipelago and Majapahit begins to disintegrate; Bali becomes a haven for Hindu-Buddhists from Java.

1500 Golden Age for Bali under King Waturenggong; first Dutch arrive in Bali (1597).

1600 Dutch East India Company sets up trading post in Batavia (Jakarta), West Java; civil war breaks out in Bali (1651); rebellion ends and Klungkung (Semarapura) founded (1681).

1700 Bali fractures into rival kingdoms, leading to continuous warfare; Bali expands control to East Java and Lombok.

1839 Danish trader Mads Lange opens a trading port at Kuta.

1849 North Bali conquered through Dutch military force.

1894–96 Karangasem dynasty in Lombok and East Bali submits to the Dutch.

1898 Dutch suppress threats to Gianyar from other kingdoms and take control of it.

1900 Dutch defeat royal families of Badung and Tabanan (1906) and Klungkung (1908). New artistic developments appear during the 1920s and 1930s, with visiting artists, anthropologists and musicians.

1917 Devastating earthquake hits Bali.

1927 Sukarno establishes Indonesia's first major political party.

1942–45 Japanese Occupation during World War II; declaration of Republic of Indonesia on 17 August 1945, after Japanese surrender.

1945–49 Dutch establish State of Eastern Indonesia that includes Bali; after war of independence, the United Nations recognises sovereignty of Indonesia, and Bali becomes a province.

1963 Mount Gunung Agung erupts, causing thousands of deaths and destroying many temples and villages.

1966 Suharto replaces Sukarno as president of Indonesia.

1976 Tourism soars with nearly 500,000 visitors.

1986 Nusa Dua developed into a high-class tourist resort area.

1990 Over one million tourists visit Bali.

1998 Asian economic crisis severely affects Indonesia; riots in Jakarta leave over 500 dead, and President Suharto resigns amid violent demonstrations; tourism to Bali suffers.

1999 Several days of rioting when Megawati Sukarnoputri, favoured Balinese candidate for president, is not selected; situation returns to normal when she becomes vice-president. Many visitors and residents of other islands seek refuge on Bali when regional conflicts erupt.

Left: a local *gamelan* band

Bali

10 km / 6 miles

The South
& Southwest

Bali is small but mountainous with deep ravines, so other than coastal routes and a few interior roads winding up and down the mountainsides, getting around takes time and will involve some backtracking, depending on where you are staying. The itineraries in this book are arranged in geographic rather than administrative regions, using the main tourist areas as your base. While the itineraries can be done in any order in a region, a circular route is most efficient for covering most of the island – and avoids time-consuming backtracking.

As a good number of temples are visited in these itineraries, it's a good idea to buy a temple sash, which you are required to wear before entering a temple. However, most temples will loan you one for a fee. Note: For place names, Pura refers to 'Temple', Danau to 'Lake', and Gunung to 'Mount'.

Southern Highlights

From the mountainous north down to the Bukit peninsula in the south, the kingdom of Mengwi, with its extensive rice fields and ties to the kingdom of Buleleng, grew in prestige, wealth and power in the 18th century. In the 19th century, however, Mengwi's powers waned, torn apart by internal strife, along with hostile attacks by its rivals. Its territories were divided between the kingdoms of Badung, with a thriving port at Kuta, and Tabanan, which became the new 'rice basket' of Bali.

Balinese rule came to a violent end in 1906, with the Dutch massacre of the Denpasar ruling house in Badung, for its king had refused to pay compensation for the supposed looting of valuables from a wrecked ship off Sanur. This was soon followed by the fall of Tabanan. Its king and crown prince, rather than face the same fate as Badung, sought a peace settlement with the Dutch. However, they were arrested for not co-operating during the embargo against Badung, and killed themselves in prison. The strategic position of the south ensured rapid growth when the Dutch moved the island's administrative centre from Singaraja in the north to Denpasar.

Today, Bali's capital city is the most densely populated and cosmopolitan area on the island, a place to stop but not to stay. The international airport is located close to major tourist centres, all with ample facilities. Kuta and Legian are crowded and noisy, famous for their beaches, shopping and nightlife, with a wide range of restaurants and accommodations for holiday-makers. Nearby, Seminyak and the stretch along the coast into Tabanan offer luxury resorts in picturesque rural settings for the more sophisticated.

Jimbaran has a beautiful curved beach and is aimed towards high-end tourism. Nusa Dua and Tanjung

Left: Bali is a surfer's haven
Right: Puputan memorial in Denpasar

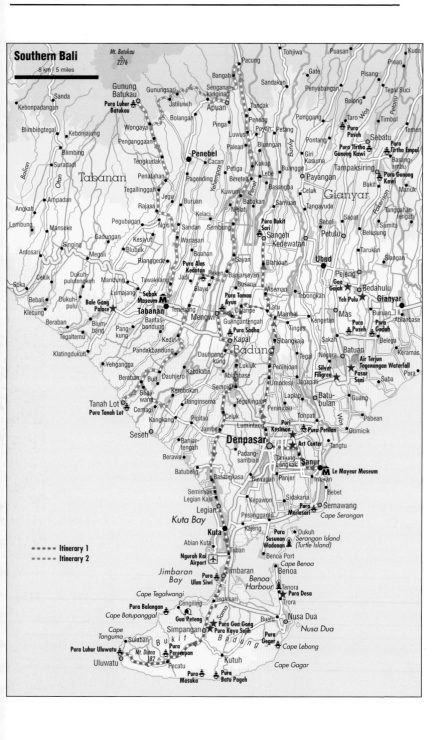

Right: the Le Mayeur Museum

Benoa, on the dry and isolated peninsula, are well-serviced luxury resort areas with fairly good beaches. From here, it is easy to take cruises to nearby islands offshore. Sanur is protected by a coral reef, so the beach is mediocre, but its relaxed and romantic atmosphere appeals to upscale tourists.

1. SANUR, DENPASAR AND ULUWATU *(see map, p22)*

Drop by an expatriate artist's beachfront home, watch music and dance classes, and visit museums and markets. Mingle with monkeys, marvel at a floating temple and see some unusual shrines. Watch sunset from a temple perched on a cliff.

If you are into horticulture in a big way do this tour on either Tuesday or Friday when the Bali Hyatt in Sanur conducts tours of its gardens at 10am.

Sanur is synonymous with gracious living, peace and solitude. In the 1930s, Sanur was little more than a tucked-away beach with nary a hotel to its name. Today, the beachfront is laced with a string of medium-range and luxury hotels and the access roads are lined with numerous art shops. Sanur's waters are calm and shallow, offering safe swimming and windsurfing at high tide; when the tide is low, however, the water almost disappears, leaving great swatches of mud and coral stretching for hundreds of kilometres out to the distant reef.

If you must have breakfast by the beach, have it at Sanur's **Bali Hyatt**, after which you can stroll around in its gardens, one of the largest and loveliest in all of Bali. Designed by transplanted Autralian landscape designer Made Wijaya, it is a sight to behold. After breakfast, visit the **Museum Le Mayeur** (Sun–Fri 8.30am–2pm; admission fee) on Sanur beach north of the Grand Bali Beach Hotel. Belgian artist Adrien-Jean Le Mayeur de Merpres (1880–1958) arrived in Bali in 1932 and married the beautiful dancer, Ni Polok, who was his only model and appeared numerous times, always bare-breasted, in his colourful Impressionistic-like paintings.

Before he died, Le Mayeur donated his studio-house with its few remaining works to the government, which was then turned into a museum managed by Ni Polok until her death in 1986. Unfortunately, the brackish sea air has taken a corrosive toll on the paintings, but the house still has an air of nostalgia and romance lingering about it.

Arts Around Town

From Sanur, take the main road into **Denpasar** for 6km (3¾ miles) and drop by the **Taman Werdhi Budaya Art Centre** (Tues–Sun 9am–4pm; admission fee), with an impressive collection of traditional and modern Balinese art, including Barong and Rangda dance costumes. From mid-June to July, the annual Bali Arts Festival takes place here with daily performances, along with displays of arts and crafts from all over the island.

Right next door is **Sekolah Tinggi Seni Indonesia** (STSI, Indonesian Arts College) on Jalan Nusa Indah, where you may be able to watch classes in Balinese music, dance and puppetry (no lessons on Saturday and Sunday). Check in at the administrative office first before wandering around. The campus also has an immense museum of different *gamelan* musical instruments and a large gallery of contemporary works by students in the visual arts programme. Both are usually closed, but try to ask someone to unlock the doors for you.

Head 2km (1¼ miles) west into the city and off Jalan Surapati, take a left turn to **Museum Bali** (Sun–Fri 8am–2pm; Fri–Sat 8–11:30am; admission fee). Established in 1932 by German artist Walter Spies (1895–1942) for the preser-

vation of traditional Balinese arts and crafts, objects are displayed in several pavilions from different parts of the island. A hall near the entrance occasionally has temporary art exhibitions.

Next door to the museum is **Pura Jagatnatha**, a modern temple dedicated to the lord of the universe. There is not much to see inside, so look through its gate at the towering white stone *padmasana* (lotus throne) topped by the gilded relief image of Sanghyang Widhi Wasa, the single supreme deity of Balinese Hinduism. This temple embodies the importance given to monotheism as promoted by the Indonesian government.

Across the street is **Lapangan Puputan Badung**, a big field with a large bronze statue of an adult and two children going to battle armed with bamboo staves, spears and and *kris*. The image was built to commemorate the *puputan* (suicide-massacre) of the city's royal families by the Dutch in 1906. Drive (or walk) 1km (½ mile) west to Jalan Sulawesi, lined with textile shops, to Jalan Gajah Mada and pause for lunch at **Atoom Baru** with its noisy atmosphere and good Chinese seafood.

Next, head for the nearby **Pasar Kumbasari** and **Pasar Badung**, the biggest marketplaces in Bali, along opposite banks of the polluted Tukad Badung River. Amidst the thousands of stalls in the sprawling multi-level complexes, you can buy anything from food and clothes to crafts and offerings. It's a non-stop bustling world of fascinating sights and smells.

Return to your car and head a short distance to the main intersection guarded by the towering **Caturmukha** statue with the faces of four differ-

Above: Balinese art at Taman Werdhi Budaya Art Centre

ent Hindu gods facing each direction: Mahadeva (west), Vishnu (north), Ishvara (east) and Brahma (south).

Head north onto Jalan Veteran and gaze at **Hotel Natour Bali**, running since the 1930s and still exuding some nostalgic charm. Further up is **Pasar Satria**, a market on the right (east) side of the street, where all kinds of tropical birds and fish and other creatures, including fighting crickets, are for sale.

A Trio of Temples

Continue north and head out of the city via Jalan Nangka, up into the mountains for a 20-km (12½-mile) scenic drive passing through **Blahkiuh**, with a huge holy banyan tree on the east side of the town's main crossroad, to **Sangeh**. This is home to hundreds of monkeys in Bali's only forest of nutmeg trees. In the middle sits the 17th-century **Pura Bukit Sari** temple. The place is usually packed with tour groups, however.

It's believed that the monkeys are descended from the lost troops of Hanuman's army from the *Ramayana* epic. Be forewarned that they are rather vicious animals, attacking tourists and taking things from them, so hide your spectacles, jewellery (remove earrings to avoid torn earlobes), and hang on tightly to your camera and bag.

Drive back down the main road for 6km (3¾ miles) south and take the right turn-off going 6km (3¾ miles) west through Penarungan to **Mengwi**, where you can gaze upon **Pura Taman Ayun**. This beautiful 'Foremost Garden Temple', appearing to float because of a surrounding moat, was built in the 18th century as a Mengwi royal family shrine. The layout represents heaven, where celestial maidens and deified ancestors relax and play. Tourists are not allowed inside, so admire the many graceful multi-roofed *meru* (pagodas) towering above the walls like the lofty masts of a huge ship. During its temple festival, processions of tall offerings come from many villages near and far (see *Calendar of Events, pages 83–5*).

Continue 3km (1¾ miles) south to Beringkit and look for the sign marking the road to **Pura Sadha**. This 18th-century 'Tower

Above: colourful Denpasar market
Right: playful monkeys at Sangeh

Temple' has an 11-tiered pagoda of brick and stone, a shrine housing three stone seats, and 54 smaller outdoor stone seats arranged in the middle of the inner courtyard. These unusual structures are said to represent a Javanese king's funerary tower that was placed in a boat with three leaders and 54 followers, but they all became stranded at sea.

A Cliff Hanger

Head back to the main road and head south 55km (34 miles) through Sempidi, Kerobokan, Kuta and Jimbaran all the way to the **Bukit** peninsula and **Pura Luhur Uluwatu**. Originally constructed during the 11th century, this 'Lofty Headstone Temple' juts out like the bow of a ship over the ocean. It was rebuilt by the Hindu priest Danghyang Nirartha, who came to Bali from Java in the 16th century following the spread of Islam there.

It was from this dramatic and narrow cliff top that he ascended into heaven after completing this last architectural wonder. A small shrine with a statue of the priest and flanked by images of Brahma and Vishnu, Hindu gods of creation and life, are in the walled section to the left just as you enter. The temple has two unusual gates, one a *candi bentar* (split gate) with relief carvings of birds and topped by curved wings, and the other an arched structure with a monster face. Both gates are guarded on each side by two statues of Ganesha, the elephant-headed Hindu lord of obstacles. Because of its location, only very hard greyish-white coral and limestone have been used.

A part of this long and narrow temple broke away and fell into the sea during the early 1900s, it is said, in premonition of the impending Dutch massacre of Badung's royal family who maintained it. Numerous repairs were made several times over the years, most recently in the late 1990s after the shrines were struck by lightning. Many people interpreted this as an omen of the immense changes arising from the Asian economic crisis.

The place is usually deserted except on full-moon nights and festival days, when crowds of Balinese come to meditate or pray (see *Calendar of Events, pages 83–5*). The views at sunset are spectacular, with fishing boats dotting the Indian Ocean and turtles swimming in the turbulent waters below. There are also some daring acrobatic monkeys on the premises.

Return along the main road leading back to the tourist centres. Stop by **Jimbaran** and feast on delicious grilled fresh seafood at the numerous night foodstalls right on the beach between the Four Seasons Resort and the Bali Intercontinental hotel.

2. FROM TANAH LOT TO BATUKAU *(see map, p22)*

Start with a visit to a coastal temple, then journey up into the mountains; after lunch, view some breathtaking scenery. Continue up to a royal temple complex before descending.

Rent a four-wheel-drive vehicle with good brakes, as the roads are quite steep and twisting. Take extra caution during the rainy season (November–March).

Start early for this long and scenic journey to **Gunung Batukau**, known as the 'Stone Coconut Shell Mountain' with its inverted *kau* or *karu* (coconut shell) profile towering at the height of 2,276m (7,467ft), making it the second highest peak in Bali.

From wherever you are staying, first drive to Kerobokan and then take the road 13km (8 miles) going west to Beraban. Turn left and travel 3km (1¾ miles) south towards the coast to **Pura Tanah Lot**. Visiting the temple at this unusually early hour means that you will be avoiding the bus-loads of noisy tourists that almost always arrive before sunset to view this stunning temple silhouetted against the twilight sky.

The Land in the Sea

This small 'Temple of the Land in the Sea' sits on a large rocky outcropping just offshore and becomes surrounded by water during high tide. A plan to build a footbridge to it a few years ago was rejected, but dozens of souvenir stalls line the pathway down to the beach.

Pura Tanah Lot is one of the most important sea temples in Bali, and people from all over the island come here to pray, especially during its festival (see *Calendar of Events, pages 83–5*). The temple was built during the 16th century by the legendary Hindu priest, Danghyang Nirartha, who left his home in Java as its population was converting to Islam.

Arriving in Bali, he wandered about and followed a mysterious glow that came from this spot. Inspired by its natural beauty, he spent the night in meditation. Some local inhabitants bothered him, so he moved the land he was on into the sea, giving the name to the place.

When he departed, he told the people to build a temple here to com-

Top Left: windswept Bukit peninsula coastline
Left: Pura Luhur Uluwatu **Right:** Pura Tanah Lot

memorate his visit. He also left behind his sash, which turned into poisonous sea snakes. These snakes are found living in caves and rocks around the base of the outcropping, said to be guarding the temple against intruders – be very careful if you try to cross over. Otherwise, be content with the view from the beach as the thundering waves crash behind the temple.

Another nearby coastal temple worth a visit is **Pura Batu Bolong**. To get there, walk northwards on the beach and you'll soon see it – resting upon an arched rocky outcrop with an opening below as rough waters surge through.

Monkeys & Terraces

Return to Beraban but continue going inland on a road that winds 9km (5½ miles) through scenic rice fields and small villages to **Kediri**. Drive north for another 5km (3 miles) and turn right on a road that takes you a short distance east to **Pura Alas Kedaton**.

Known as the 'Temple of the Royal Forest', the temple complex has many monkeys and fruit bats living in surrounding trees. Helpful guides will show you around for a small fee. Backtrack to the main road and go 2km (1¼ miles) uphill before turning right and travelling the same distance east to **Blayu**, where beautiful hand-woven cloths are made.

Continue further east for another 1km (½ mile), and turn left onto the very good paved main road going 24km (15 miles) uphill to **Pacung**. Stop at **Pacung Cottages** and have lunch at its restaurant overlooking spectacular rice terraces.

The best is yet to come. Take the narrow winding road going 13km (8 miles) west through steep rice terraces to **Jatiluwih**. True to its name, which means 'extraordinary', this scenic point offers some of the most breathtaking views in Bali. Take some time to enjoy the grand and stunning scenery that unfolds before you.

Above: scenic rice terraces at Pacung
Left: *garuda* image at Pura Luhur Batukau

A Sacred Sanctuary

Continue along the road for 4km (2½ miles) to **Wongaya**, and turn right on the main road that continues for another 2km (1¼ miles) to **Pura Luhur Batukau**. This 'Lofty Stone Coconut Shell Temple' complex is located about halfway up the mountain slopes of Gunung Batukau.

This was the ancestral temple for the royal family of Tabanan, whose descendants still maintain the shrines till today. Two smaller temples, **Pura Dalem** and **Pura Panyaum**, are found on the lower level. The main enclosure is at the higher mountain end, with several multiple-tiered *meru* (pagodas) for the deified kings.

On the eastern side is an artificial pond with two shrines in the middle. One is for the goddess of Danau Tamblingan, the other is for the god of Gunung Batukau, thus representing the concept of *rwa bhineda* (cosmic duality), the Balinese equivalent of Chinese *yin-yang* philosophy.

This ancient sacred site was renovated and landscaped in 1991, however, taking away some of its original mystique. It is still a quiet and beautiful place to wander around in, but streams of worshippers bearing offerings come from afar to pray during its festival (see *Calendar of Events, pages 83–5*).

Descend 8km (5 miles) back down the main road to **Penatahan**, where you can have a relaxing soak after a long day in **Yeh Panes**, a natural hot spring. Natural phenomena that are unusual, such as hot springs, are believed to be frequented by spirits and so Yeh Panes is graced by a small temple where people make offerings with prayers. The springs are part of a modest hot springs resort but non-guests can utilise the spa for a fee. Take the left turn-off going south-east for 4km (2½ miles) until it joins the main road heading 10km (6¼ miles) south through Wanasari and all the way down to Tabanan. From here it's an easy 13km (8 miles) drive to Sempidi, where major roads lead back to the main tourist centres.

3. NUSA LEMBONGAN AND NUSA PENIDA (see map, p31)

Get away to a small island off the southeast coast for watersports and explore small fishing villages. On another larger island, visit a temple renowned for its practitioners of black magic, and take a trip around to see some natural wonders.

If snorkelling and watersports is all you have in mind, book yourself on a half-day trip at your hotel. If you are an intrepid explorer, plan to stay the night or longer.

Although Nusa Lembongan and Nusa Penida (along with the tiny uninhabited Nusa Ceningan) are part of the region of Klungkung, these offshore islands are more accessible on pleasure cruises leaving from **Tanjung Benoa** harbour in **Badung** (see *Practical Information, page 98*). If you go by cheaper or public boats from Sanur, Kusamba or Padangbai, the crossing can be rough and slow, even danger-

Right: Nusa Penida beach

ous depending on sea conditions. You can charter your own vessel from these places, but this may end up being more expensive and slower and riskier than a commercial cruise.

Underwater & Underground

Most pleasure boats take visitors to **Nusa Lembongan** on packaged day tours, about 26km (16 miles) from Tanjung Benoa for excellent diving and snorkelling around coral reefs in the pristine waters of an idyllic bay.

If you want to stay for a few days, take a luxury catamaran trip on **Wakalouka Cruises** (tel: 0361-426972) to the luxury **Wakanusa Resort** (tel: 0361-723629). Accommodations for independent travellers are also available

at **Agung Bungalows**, **Nusa Lembongan Resort** (tel: 0361-725864) and **Wayan Tarci Homestay**.

Most visitors swim, snorkel and nap for most of the day, as the weather can get very hot and dry. If the cruise you are on allows time for it, in the mid-afternoon, walk to the main village of **Jungut Batu**, with its sandy compounds and squat pavilions surrounded by thick and low coral or limestone walls.

Just over 1km (½ mile) to the south is **Lembongan**, a fishing village with seaweed farms. Pause on the hilltop along the way, where, on a clear day, there are stunning views across Badung Strait to Bali, with Gunung Agung rising 3,142m (10,300ft) dramatically from the sea.

At **Jenggut Batu** on the other side of the hill, visit **Rumah di Bawah Tanah**, a bizarre underground house built over 40 years ago by a local priest acting upon divine inspiration. The multiple tunnels, nooks and crannies carved out from limestone can be rather eerie. Give a donation to the late priest's family if you visit this oddity.

Return to your lodging or boat before sunset, as the paths are not lit at night.

Centre of Sorcery

If you stay overnight on Nusa Lembongan, get a boat to take you early the next morning to **Nusa Penida**, the largest of the three islands. There is little infrastructure and accommodation, so try to do what you can in one day and then head back to Nusa Lembongan.

During the 18th and 19th centuries, the kingdom of Klungkung sent its undesirables and criminals into exile on Nusa Penida. In spite of this dubious background, the people are quite friendly and welcome visitors to their remote 'Limestone Island'. Nusa Penida is famous for its *kain cepuk*, a hand-woven *ikat* (weft tie-dyed) cloth with complex and multi-coloured geometric patterns on a red or maroon background. This textile has power-

Above: Nusa Lembongan has quaint villages and good reefs for snorkellers ful magical properties and is worn by Rangda, the widow-witch of Balinese exorcist drama (see *History & Culture, pages 14–6*).

Otherwise, life is hard on Nusa Penida, with most people earning their living by fishing, trading and cultivating seaweed. There are few opportunities for education and employment. A proposal to turn the island into a legalised gambling centre a few years ago was rejected.

There are also settlers from Java, Lombok and Sulawesi in the main town of **Toya Pakeh**. Pack along lunch or snacks and lots of bottled water, then hire a vehicle with driver for the day to first take you 3km (1¾ miles) east to **Pura Dalem Peed** (pronounced 'puh-aid'), the most important temple in Bali for practitioners of black magic. Worshippers from all over Bali come here to pray during its festival (see *Calendar of Events, pages 83–5*).

Be sure to ask permission from the priests before entering, and don't forget to give a small donation before leaving. As befits its reputation, the atmosphere is rather spooky. Growing inside the temple is a strange tangle of three different trees, forming a great twisted mass.

The patron deity here is Ratu Gede Mas Mecaling, the 'Fanged Lord of Victims' who flies to Bali with his invisible troops as balls of fire to spread disease and pestilence during the hot and rainy season from November to March. The Balinese repel them with the lord's own fearsome image in the *barong landung* (tall puppet figures) of Jero Gede and his wife, Jero Luh, whose smiling faces appear to be rather Chinese.

Several other places on the island are worth visiting. Drive 10km (6¼ miles) along the northeast coast to see the cave of **Goa Karangsari**, a good place to escape from the midday heat. Continue south up into the hills and then northwest for 16km (10 miles) to **Sebuluh** waterfall near Batumadeg, an unusual sight in such a dry place. Finally, head north back to Toyapakeh for a boat to Nusa Lembongan for another night or return to Bali.

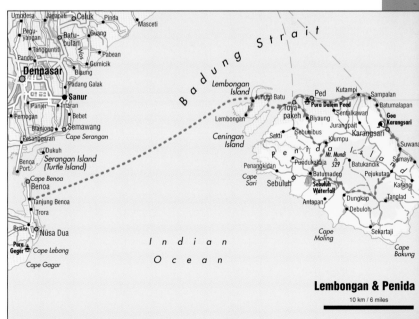

Lembongan & Penida

10 km / 6 miles

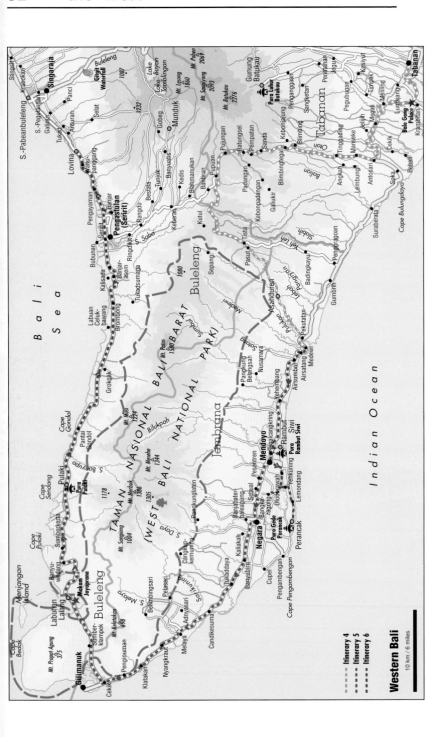

Western Bali

- ▪▪▪▪ Itinerary 4
- •••• Itinerary 5
- ──── Itinerary 6

10 km / 6 miles

The West

I t is ironical that the west, where the oldest remains of civilisation were found on Bali, is today the most uninhabited part of the island. Prehistoric human remains discovered here are related to those in neighbouring Java, when the two islands were joined during the Ice Age. The Bali Strait, less than 4km (2½ miles) wide and only 60m (200 ft) deep, now separates them.

The Balinese tell the story of Empu Siddhimantra, a Javanese priest who went to Bali's Gunung Agung to seek the help of Basuki, the underworld serpent of wealth, to pay off the gambling debt of his son, Manik Angkeran. Basuki granted them jewels and gold, but one day, the greedy young son cut off a huge jewel from Basuki's tail and fled with it. Angered, the serpent burnt him to ashes. Later, however, Siddhimantra restored Basuki's jewel and the serpent brought the youth back to life. Siddhimantra then ordered his descendants to remain forever in Bali and serve Basuki. To keep them there, he scraped a line in the ground with the end of his walking stick in the narrowest part of land on his way back. The sea flowed in, forming the Bali Strait to separate Java from Bali.

The shallow and narrow waters, however, did not prevent the Javanese from invading Bali in the 14th century. Two brother princes from the kingdom of Gelgel were sent to settle in West Bali during the 15th century, but rivalry grew between them, and they ended up killing each other.

The area rose again after the fall of Gelgel during the 17th century and due to the weakness of the Klungkung kingdom, a leader in West Bali declared himself king of the 'Jimbar Forest', Jimbarwana or Jembrana, in the 18th century. However, it was soon conquered by the more powerful Buleleng kingdom.

After 1920, the Dutch encouraged transmigration from other parts of Bali to populate this remote area. Some Balinese, expelled from their villages for converting to Christianity, also moved here during the 1930s. Catholics settled at Pulasari and Protestants at Blimbingsari.

Also among the inhabitants are Muslim Balinese, Javanese, Madurese, Buginese from Sulawesi, even Malays from Trengganu. There is one mosque to every five Balinese Hindu temples. Most people are farmers and fishermen.

West Bali remains sparsely populated, with the majority living in the regional capital of Negara. Much of the land is a protected nature reserve, which also limits the number of inhabitants and restricts tourist developments to the coast. West Bali is ideal for those who are interested in eco-tourism and want to get away from the city altogether.

Right: big Balinese smiles

4. Krambitan, Pupuan & Medewi *(see map, p32)*

Visit two palaces, then head to the mountains for spectacular views. Drive through clove plantations and a hole in a tree, then relax on a beach at sunset.

If you are already in West Bali and heading towards the south, doing this route in reverse order prevents backtracking and saves time.

After breakfast, get your hotel to pack you a picnic lunch. Drive 4km (2½ miles) west past the city of Tabanan until you come to a left turn-off at

Penyalin. Continue south-west 5km (3 miles) to **Krambitan**. A part of the Tabanan region, this royal town has two palaces, the older **Puri Gede** and the newer **Puri Anyar**, both with beautiful architecture.

The royal families support traditional Balinese literature and still keep precious collections of *lontar* (dried palm leaf) manuscripts. Artists here also create a local style of *wayang* (puppet figure) painting.

Krambitan is famous for *tektekan*, an exciting rendition of the *Calonarang* exorcist drama (see *History & Culture, pages 14–6*) with trance performed to the rhythmic beating of bamboo tubes and wooden bells. Another dance is *leko* or *andir*, a form of *legong* with trance by young girls in nearby Tista.

Views & an Unusual Tree

From Krambitan, go north 5km (3 miles) through Belong and Dukuhgede back to the main road at Meliling. Turn left and drive 10km (6¼ miles) west to Antosari, then turn right and begin a scenic 37-km (23-mile) drive up the mountains to **Pupuan**. Stop for a picnic lunch and spectacular views of rice terraces as far as the eye can see.

From here, head 13km (8 miles) west on a winding road to Pertigaan, then turn left to go 6km (3¾ miles) downhill to Tista. Continue 10km (6¼ miles) through clove plantations in **Asahduren**. Look for trim spice trees with orange tipped leaves. You might see and smell fragrant buds drying on mats by roadsides.

From here, it's 11km (6¾ miles) down to the coast. Along the way, you'll drive through **Bunut Bolong**, a gigantic *bunut*, a type of banyan tree, with the road going through a hole in its base. When the road was built, it was decided not to cut down such a huge and powerful tree due to the spirit living in it, so the road went through its mammoth trunk instead. A shrine nearby with colourful tiger figures has been built for the wayward local spirits to reside in. Just beyond the tree is an overlook with views of the expansive and forested mountains of western Bali.

On the coastal route, continue west to **Medewi** and watch the sun set at this black-sand beach, popular with surfers. Nearby, there is a good hotel (see *Practical Information on page 96*). Be careful of the strong currents and waves here if you decide to swim.

Above: a *legong* dancer with palms clasped together to show respect
Right: bull-racing in Negara

5. WESTERN HIGHLIGHTS *(see map, p32)*

Drop by some seaside temples, explore a nature reserve, visit the grave of a folk hero and soak in some hot springs.

If you do not want to visit West Bali National Park, then after this journey, continue on with Itinerary 6. If you are coming from the north, then doing this route in reverse prevents backtracking and saves time.

After breakfast, pack along a picnic lunch. From Medewi beach, go west 20km (12½ miles) along the main road until you see a sign on the left for the turn-off to **Pura Rambut Siwi**, perched on a seaside cliff. When the Javanese priest Danghyang Nirartha came to Bali to seek refuge from Islam in the 16th century, he used his powers to put an end to a plague that was ravaging the people here. The people wanted him to stay, but Nirartha wanted to leave, so he left behind something of his instead – a strand of hair that was enshrined in this 'Temple of The Lock of Hair'. Further down on the beach is **Pura Segara**, a sea temple and home to an invisible tiger spirit.

Bamboo & Bulls

Continue 7km (4¼ miles) west on the main road to **Tegalcangkring**, a village known for its *jegog* ensembles of giant bamboo xylophones. Just beyond, turn left at Mendoyo towards the sea and continue 10km (6¼ miles) along the coast to **Perancak**, where **Taman Rekreasi Perancak** (Perancak Recreational Park; daily 9am–5pm; admission fee) has a small zoo and a field for *makepung* (bull races). Bull-racing was introduced by Madurese migrants. Two bulls, decorated with bells and colourful cloths, pull a two-wheeled chariot with a standing jockey. Races take place in villages after the rice harvests (September–October), with regional competitions held in Negara.

Nearby is **Pura Gede Perancak**, where Javanese priest Danghyang Nirartha first landed in Bali during the 16th century. He sat to rest under an *ancak* (a kind of banyan tree), explaining the name of the place.

Backtrack 7km (4¼ miles) and take a left turn-off north to Yehkuning

and up 5km (3 miles) to **Sangkaragung**, another village that plays music on giant bamboo xylophones. You can both hear and feel the sounds and vibrations when several groups compete in *jegog mebarung* contests.

Dances based on *pencak silat* (self-defence) can be done to this exciting music. In *kendang mebarung*, drummers compete by beating giant drums. Another ensemble is *bumbung gebyog*, in which the ends of different lengths of bamboo are beaten rhythmically on a board.

National Parks & Shrines

Continue 8km (5 miles) west to the wealthy town of **Negara**, but there's not much to see or do in the regional capital. Follow the main coastal road northwest for 50km (31 miles) to **Cekik**, site of the oldest remains of human civilisation on Bali.

At the **Taman Nasional Bali Barat** (West Bali National Park) headquarters (Mon–Thur 8am–2pm; Fri 8–11am; Sat 8am–1pm) are displays of artefacts excavated from nearby prehistoric sites. Apply here for the permit and guide needed to visit this 192,000-acre (77,700-ha) protected nature reserve. Established in 1984, the park is one of Bali's few remaining pristine areas. It is home to several species of deer, civets, monkeys and the rare wild Javan buffalo, of which just a few dozens remain. It is also home to the nearly-extinct Bali starling (also known as Rothschild's mynah). In their efforts to preserve this species, zoos around the world have sent specimens back to Bali to increase the available gene pool in a vigorous breeding programme. To explore this huge reserve, stay overnight at Banyuwedang (see below) and continue the next day.

A further 21km (13 miles) east in Teluk Terima is **Makam Jayaprana**, a grave-shrine with a glass case containing modern figures of a Balinese couple. In a Balinese folktale set in North Bali, a handsome orphaned youth named Jayaprana was adopted by the Lord of Kalianget (near Lovina). When Jayaprana married the lovely maiden Layonsari, the lord became jealous and wanted her for himself. He sent Jayaprana on a false mission and had his soldiers murder the innocent youth and bury him at Teluk Terima.

Layonsari refused to submit to the evil lord and committed suicide to join Jayaprana in death. The lord went insane and murdered members of his court until his own soldiers killed him.

Today, women bring offerings to the shrine and pray for divine assistance. A person whose wish is granted brings a clock; the great number of timepieces here show that many have been helped.

Follow the road for 10km (6¼ miles) to **Banyuwedang** (daily 9am–6pm, admission), literally 'Hot Water' for its natural hot springs with healing properties. There are hotels here and in Pemuteran 10km (6¼ miles) further east.

Left: West Bali National Park

6. FROM PULAKI TO THE NORTH *(see map, p32)*

Dive among reefs full of tropical fish, then visit two temples with fascinating origins. Drop by a Buddhist monastery and relax in a hot springs before ending at a coastal resort.

If you are already in Lovina, then reverse the order of this itinerary. If you do not want to visit Pulau Menjangan, then continue on with Itinerary 5 in reverse order, which prevents backtracking and saves time.

Both **Mimpi Resort** in Banyuwedang and **Matahari Beach Resort** in Pemuteran, further east *(see Practical Information, page 96)* can get you the required permit, arrange the boat trip from Labuhan Lalang, and rent equipment for snorkelling or diving in reefs full of colourful fish around **Pulau Menjangan** (Deer Island), part of Taman Nasional Bali Barat (West Bali National Park). The diving here is considered to be unsurpassed in all of Bali, with good visibility, numerous caves and a spectacular drop-off.

Located off the northwest tip of Bali, Deer Island got its name when the Javanese holy man, Empu Kuturan, arrived here during the 10th or 11th century. A deer led him or let him ride on its back, all the way to Pura Besakih on Gunung Agung. Today, the rare Java deer is rarely seen, but the island is a protected sanctuary for the Bali starling.

Land of Invisible Beings

After the island excursion, take time for lunch and then travel 11km (6¾ miles) east from Banyuwedang past Pemuteran to **Pulaki**. A village famous for grapes, arbours heavy with vines rise up everywhere. There are also several natural hot springs nearby.

During the 16th century, the priest Danghyang Nirartha left Java with his family and followers because of the growing influence of Islam there. He came here to Bali with them but went off to meditate alone elsewhere.

While Nirartha was away, some local men violated his lovely young daughter. Upon returning and learning about this, the priest cursed all the vil-

Above: dive equipment at Menjangan island

lagers to become invisible as *wong gamang* or *wong samar*. Sometimes they are seen by humans and are recognisable by their cleft lips, giving them tiger-like appearances.

Even their village became invisible, so they lived at **Pura Pulaki**, a temple built on a rocky cliff. The violated daughter could not face mortal life anymore, so Nirartha also made her invisible. She became deified as Dewi Melanting, goddess of the marketplace, and is enshrined at the nearby **Pura Dalem Melanting**. Beware of the aggressive monkeys that inhabit these places.

From Buddha to Bathing

If you want to do more swimming and snorkelling, go 10km (6¼ miles) east to the pretty **Pantai Gondol**. Another 21km (13 miles) east along the coastal road is **Labuan Celukbawang**, a port built to replace the old one in Singaraja. You may even see a traditional Buginese schooner from Sulawesi.

Drive 16km (10 miles) further east to Seririt, a town that was rebuilt after it was completely destroyed by an earthquake in 1976. There's nothing much to see or do here, so head 4km (2½ miles) east to **Banjar** and follow the sign to the striking **Brahma Vihara Arama** monastery located 2km (1¼ miles) up a steep hillside.

This modern Theravada Buddhist monastery was built by a Balinese Buddhist monk in 1971 and replaced the older one founded in 1958. Inside is a gilded Thai Buddha image. The place is closed for 10 days in April and

September for meditation retreats. Dress respectfully, speak softly, and remove your shoes to enter.

Follow the narrow road further to **Air Panes** (daily 9am–6pm; admission fee), a natural hot spring set in a pleasant landscaped environment. In 1985, the tepid 38°C sulfuric waters, believed to cure skin ailments, was channelled to pour out of carved serpent spouts into three levels of pools. There are showers, toilets and changing rooms so have a relaxing soak before heading on to Lovina.

Tonight, give yourself a treat by making reservations at the Damai Lovina Villas restaurant (tel: 362-41008), located on the mountain slopes just outside of Lovina. A Paul Bocuse-trained Danish chef whips up exciting dishes using fresh Balinese ingredients and produce.

Above: Lovina's bountiful grape harvest
Left: Brahma Vihara Arama monastery

The North

the north

With rugged volcanic mountains dividing Bali from east to west and forming a natural barrier, North Bali developed a different culture and character from the south. The long north coast and the calm Bali Sea exposed the area to outside trade influences from India, China, Southeast Asia and the West. With a drier climate, less irrigation and fewer gentle slopes for wet rice cultivation, North Bali is more suitable for fruit and coffee growing. Still, the best quality Balinese rice comes from this region.

When civil war tore the Balinese kingdom of Gelgel apart during the 17th century, its successor, Klungkung, was too weak to control the island. In the north, Ki Gusti Ngurah Panji Sakti became very powerful and declared himself king of North Bali, calling it Buleleng. Other kingdoms rose, but during the 18th century, Buleleng conquered Jembrana in the west and formed an alliance with Mengwi in the south. Rivalry among its descendants weakened Buleleng and enabled Karangasem in the east to take over, until a rebellion in 1823 restored local rule.

In 1845, an alliance between these two former enemies made Buleleng and Karangasem a major force to contend with. The Dutch, who had been trying to get a foothold on the island for decades, wanted to put an end to this powerful realm but needed a legitimate reason in order to take action. They soon had the perfect excuse to interfere when the king of Buleleng refused to pay compensation for looting the cargo of a wrecked ship belonging to the Dutch. Military expeditions were sent in 1846 and 1848, but Buleleng was able to defeat the Dutch. Finally, a third attempt in 1849 ended with victory for the Dutch over Buleleng and Jembrana. They established their colonial centre in Singaraja, but later moved it to the south after defeating the royal families of Badung in 1906.

Until the harbour and airport opened in the south, Singaraja was the main port for trade and the arrival place for tourists. It still is an important educational centre on the island. Up to the 1920s, North Bali was the leader in music and dance, especially the flashy *kebyar* style that was popularised in the south. The popular *drama gong* (stage play) also originated here during the 1970s. Traditional ceremonial dances are still performed during temple festivals here.

Today, Buleleng is Bali's largest region and ranks second in population after Badung in the south. Its beautiful scenery, quiet beaches and mountains cover one-third of the island. North Bali also remains laid-back, having developed slower due to the concentration of tourism in the south. A long stretch of beach called Lovina is the main tourist centre, with hotels, homestays and excellent seafood. Some of the central-western mountain resort areas are also more accessible from the north.

Right: a balancing act

7. BRATAN AND BEDUGUL *(see map, p41)*

Marvel at a mountain waterfall, then visit a lakeside temple complex. Explore a botanical garden, drive around scenic lakes, and descend through mountain villages back to the coast.

If you're coming via Tabanan (see South and Southwest Bali itineraries, pages 23–31), go to Bedugul, Bratan, Tamblingan and Gitgit before coming to Lovina, but leave out Munduk.

Get an early start after breakfast. Go all the way east to **Singaraja**, *(see page 42)* turn into Jalan Veteran and continue until you see a tall statue of the winged lion **Singa Ambara Raja**, a proud symbol of the region of Buleleng. Continue to the junction that connects to Jalan Gajah Mada, turning right to drive up to the mountains.

Located 10km (6 miles) south and nearby the main road is **Air Terjun Gitgit** (daily 9am–6pm; admission fee), an impressive 40-m (131-ft) waterfall that plunges into a deep pool. A swim here can be very refreshing, but try to do it alone, as it is believed that couples bathing here together will separate. If you haven't had breakfast yet, there are restaurants at nearby hotels.

Lakeside Sites

Continue 13km (8 miles) up the cool mountains to **Pura Ulun Danu Bratan**, a large 17th-century Hindu-Buddhist temple complex set amidst landscaped gardens. Two multiple-roofed *meru* (pagodas) sit at the edge of **Danau Bratan**

and honour the lake goddess, Dewi Danu, provider of irrigation water for rice fields in the western half of Bali. The pagodas are usually surrounded by water, but the level of the lake has dropped a bit. Narrow strips of land and bamboo bridges now connect the temple to the shore.

A nearby *stupa* (memorial shrine) has four Buddhas in niches around its sides facing the four major compass points. The figures are draped in coloured cloths representing the Hindu directions, an example of religious fusion. Villagers in Bratan lean more towards Buddhism, with simpler offerings and ceremonies than those of the more Hindu-oriented followers. Although entry into the temple itself is not allowed, the surrounding view of the temple complex, beautiful gardens and the majestic but often clouded Gunung Catur is definitely worth seeing.

If the water looks more tempting, then boats and watersports equipment can be hired from nearby lakeside hotels and rental kiosks. At **Candi Kuning**, the main village with several hotels, visit the colourful flower, fruit and vegetable market. Cross the road to the **Ananda Restaurant** for lunch to try one of the best Indonesian dishes featuring fresh fish from the lake.

Above: lakeside Pura Ulun Danu
Right: children from Munduk village in North Bali

Tropical Surprise

Located west of the market in the **Bedugul** area is **Kebun Eka Raya Botanical Gardens**, definitely worth visiting. You won't feel like you're in Bali while wandering around on clearly marked paths through tropical 'alpine' forests of pine trees. The clean, crisp air is very refreshing. Take time to enjoy this 325-acre (132-ha) park, which also has a collection of orchids and even a cactus hothouse.

The cool climate made Bedugul a favourite place for the Dutch seeking escape from the heat and humidity. If you can't get enough of it and want to explore more of the extensive gardens, there are some good places for overnight stays in the area *(see Practical Information, page 96)*.

Otherwise, take the winding road over to the other two smaller lakes nearby, **Danau Buyan** and **Danau Tamblingan**. These were once a single body of water until a landslide divided them in 1818. The smaller lake, Danau Tamblingan, has a small temple down by its edge with two beautiful and airy multi-roofed *meru* (pagodas) built in the local style. Next to them is a newer and more solid-looking *meru* in the south-central architectural style.

Continue 6km (3¾ miles) to **Munduk**, a clove- and coffee-growing village overlooking rice terraces. Archaeological evidence indicate that a community was in existence in Munduk between the 10th and 14th century, until the Dutch took control of North Bali in the 1890s and turned this area into a cash crop-producing region. The road goes another 16km (10 miles) to Mayong, where it meets the main road to the coast. Turn right and go 10km (6¼ miles) to Seririt, then turn right again and return 16km (10 miles) back to Lovina.

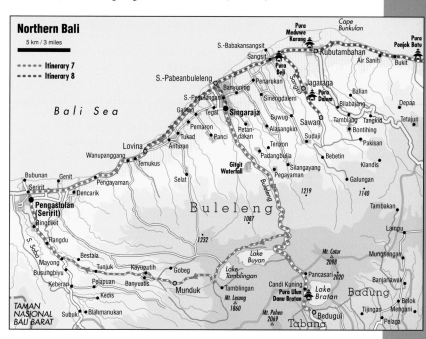

Northern Bali

5 km / 3 miles

- - - - Itinerary 7
- - - - Itinerary 8

Bali Sea

Cape Bunkulan
Pura Ponjok Batu
Pura Meduwe Karang
S.-Babakansangsit
Sangsit
Kubutambahan
Air Sanih
Bukit
Pura Beji
S.-Pabeanbuleleng
Penarukan
Banyuning
Jagaraga
Balian
Depaa
S.-Pegulangan
Sinengdalem
Pura Dalem
Bilabajang
Galrad
Tegal
Singaraja
Suwug
Sawan
Tamblang
Tangkid
Tetajun
Pemaron
Panci
Petan-dakan
Alasangkin
Sudaji
Bontihing
Pakisan
Lovina
Tukad
Anturan
Tenaon
Bebetin
Klandis
Wanupanggang
Temukus
Padangbulia
Silangayang
Galungan
Bubunan
Genit
Selat
Gitgit Waterfall
Pegayaman
1219
1140
Seririt
Pengayaman
Dencarik
Tambakan
Pengastulan (Seririt)
Ringdikit
1087
Lampu
Rangdu
1232
Mungsengan
Bestala
Lake Buyan
Mt. Catur 2098
Mayong
Tunjuk
Kayuputih
Gobeg
Lake Tamblingan
Pancasari 2020
Banjarlawak
Busungbiyu
Keberan
Pelapuan
Banyuatis
Munduk
Tamblingan
Candi Kuning
Lake Bratan
Badung
Belok
Kedis
Mt. Lesong 1860
Pura Ulun Danu Bratan
Tijingan
Mengani
TAMAN NASIONAL BALI BARAT
Subuk
Blahmanukan
Mt. Pohen 2069
Bedugul
Pelaga
Tabana

Buleleng

8. LOVINA AND SINGARAJA *(see map, p41)*

Go dolphin watching in the morning, then see sites around the old capital. Visit temples with fascinating carvings, see a musical instrument foundry, and cool off in some natural springs. After lunch, drop by another coastal temple.

If you're going next to Karangasem, this itinerary takes you to sights along the way. If you're coming from Karangasem (see East Bali itineraries, pages 46–56), do this itinerary in reverse order to get to Lovina.

Caressed by gentle waves, **Lovina** is a good, clean and safe area for swimming with long stretches of quiet black-sand beaches. Fishermen take their outrigger canoes right up to the shore to unload their catches, selling them to vendors and restaurants.

Lovina is one of two places around Bali where there are dolphins. Most hotels in this area arrange dolphin-watching excursions. Purchase tickets the night before and get up early the next morning (the boatman may actually come to your room to wake you up) for the motorised canoe ride to where the dolphins gather.

Most boatmen search for the dolphins by chasing after them, which no doubt disturbs them and the tourists. Instead, tell your boatman to just stay in one place, as the dolphins usually will come close to your drifting canoe.

The Lion King

Singaraja was Bali's capital from 1855 until the Dutch moved it south to Denpasar after defeating the royal families there in 1906. The city of the 'Lion King' still has some good examples of colonial architecture, and is a major educational and cultural centre of present-day Bali. It has two university campuses and is well known for its silver crafts and hand-woven *songket*.

Stop by **Gedong Kertya** (Tues–Thur 8am–2pm; Fri 8–11am; Sat 8am–1pm; free) on Jalan Veteran. This library was founded in 1928 by the Dutch to preserve thousands of *lontar* manuscripts. Dried fan palm leaves are inscribed with a pointed stylus and wiped with oily soot to make the lines visible. Many also have fine illustrations. Since these 'books' tend to decay over time due to insects, humidity and fungus, you might see a librarian making a new copy. The library also has a collection of old publications and Balinese paintings made before World War II. Some manuscripts and ancient inscriptions on copper plates are also on display.

Located nearby is **Puri Sinar Nadi Putra**, once a part of the former palace and now a centre for beautiful hand-woven silk textiles. From here, head 3km (1¼ miles) down Jalan Gajah Mada towards the old harbour. Most of the remaining structures on the waterfront were destroyed by high waves in the early 1990s.

There are still a few Dutch-style buildings and a Chinese *klenteng* (temple) by the shore. Visitors are usually not allowed inside, but you can peer through the gates at the interior walls that are covered with paintings of

Above: playful dolphin at Lovina

Buddhist deities and figures. The Chinese were once very active as traders in Singaraja, and there is still a high concentration of them living in the city.

Jutting out over the water's edge is **Yuddha Mandalatama**, a monument showing a soldier bearing a flag. It commemorates the Indonesian struggle for independence against the Dutch from 1945–49.

Stone Vehicles & Metal Music

Travel 8km (5 miles) east out of Singaraja to **Sangsit** for the 15th-century **Pura Beji** located just off the main road. A *subak* (irrigation) temple, its soft pink sandstone walls are embellished with very good carvings of monsters and demons that seem to emerge from the incredible main gate.

Just beyond Sangsit is a road to the right that climbs 5km (3 miles) uphill to **Jagaraga**. Formerly called Sukapura, it was renamed Jagaraga (Self-Guarding) when the king of Buleleng, Gusti Ketut Jelantik, built a fortress here to fight against the Dutch during the third military campaign in 1849. He fled the cannon bombardment but was ambushed and killed in the hills of Karangasem. The **Pura Dalem** or 'Temple of the Dead' here has interesting wall carvings of battles old and new, including two Europeans in a Ford Model T car being held up by bandits, World War II aeroplanes fighting and plunging into the sea, and a Dutch steamer signalling an SOS distress call as sea monsters attack.

Continue further up the road another 4km (2½ miles) to **Sawan**. Follow the rhythmic pounding sounds of metal to the foundry of **Pande Made Widandra**. Watch molten bronze poured into moulds and gongs hammered out for musical instruments of the Balinese *gamelan* ensemble.

Carvers here also make wooden frames for the bronze keys and kettles. Only a few visitors come this far to see them, so the workers will be happy to show you around and explain things. The village is also known for its very good dancers.

Backtrack downhill to the main road,

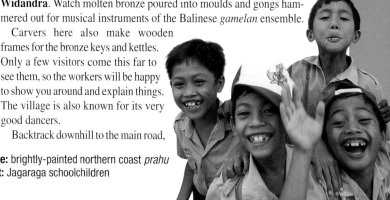

Above: brightly-painted northern coast *prahu*
Right: Jagaraga schoolchildren

then turn right and head 5km (3 miles) east to see the fascinating **Pura Maduwe Karang** at **Kubutambahan**. This 'Temple of the Land Owner' honours the deity of non-irrigated crops like coffee and corn that are commonly grown in the dry fields in the area.

There are many interesting carvings on the walls and shrines, with stone figures from the Indian *Ramayana* epic standing outside on three tiers. The most famous relief is of W O J Nieuwenkamp, a Dutch artist who rode around on his bicycle in the early 1900s, the first ever seen on Bali at the time. The fanciful flower-wheeled bicycle carving is found on a wall on the north side.

By the Sea

Continue 6km (3¾ miles) east along the main coastal road until you arrive at **Air Sanih** (daily 8am–6pm; admission fee), a large natural spring-fed pool set in pretty tropical gardens right at the edge of the sea. Fresh cold water flows out at an astonishing 800 litres per second.

Take a break for a refreshing swim, then enjoy a lunch of standard Indonesian and Chinese food at the adjoining Air Sanih Restaurant. Cross the street and climb up the stairs to **Pura Taman Manik Mas**, the 'Garden Temple of the Golden Gem' for sea breezes and views of the coast.

Continue driving 3km (1¾ miles) east until you come to **Pura Ponjok Batu**, a large seaside temple on a scenic hillside overlooking the coast, renovated in the late 1990s. During the 16th century, the Javanese priest Danghyang Nirartha stopped to admire the view at this 'Temple of the Projecting Stone' when he saw a boat in trouble. He revived its unconscious crew and took them back home to the island of Lombok, even though the mast was broken and there was no sail.

End your day by returning west 32km (20 miles) along the coast all the way back to Lovina, or continue on to Tulamben with Itinerary 9 (see *East Bali, pages 46–8*).

Above: Pura Maduwe Karang – wall relief detail of the Dutch cyclist

The East

the east

Much like the islands of East Indonesia, East Bali is a rugged area of contrasts. The great mass of the island's highest active volcano, Gunung Agung, dominates the landscape. Nestled among the foothills are lush valleys with small but dense communities. The eastern and northern parts of the region of Karangasem are dry and sparsely populated.

Between Bali and Lombok to the east are some of the deepest waters in the Indonesian archipelago, where the Asian continental shelf ends. Here lies the Wallace Line (actually more of a zone than a clearly-defined boundary) that extends north between Kalimantan and Sulawesi. The 19th-century, British naturalist Sir Alfred Wallace (1822–1913) observed that the lush islands on the west side of the Lombok Strait differed from those on the east side, which were arid with flora and fauna more like that of Australia.

In this geographical setting, the people of East Bali developed a strong sense of identity. A number of villages populated by aboriginal Bali Aga people still retain customs that survived the 14th-century Javanese conquest of the island.

Karangasem came to prominence in the early 18th century following the fall of the Balinese kingdom of Gelgel and the weak central authority of Klungkung. The kingdom quickly grew in strength, extending its influence over Buleleng in North Bali, and east to Lombok. It became so powerful in Lombok that it even helped the Dutch in their military campaigns against the kingdoms of Buleleng and Jembrana in Bali in 1849.

In 1894–96, the Karangasem dynasty in Lombok and East Bali submitted to Dutch rule after a bloody massacre of the Balinese ruling family. The dynasty retained some status and in 1938 was granted self-rule by recognising the colonial authority. Many areas of Karangasem suffered terribly during the eruption of Gunung Agung in 1963, prompting the authorities to change the royal town's name to Amlapura to avoid future disaster. However, most people still use the old name. Until roads were rebuilt recently, most of the area was untouched by tourism.

Karangasem remains less developed but is more relaxing. Today, the coastal resort town of Candi Dasa, which used to be a quiet fishing village, is the main tourist centre, with a string of hotels, restaurants and shops, and is a good place to explore the countryside. While in the northeast, also visit the artistic community of Tejakula and the salt-making villages of Tianyar and Kubu; take in the views of beautifully-sculpted rice terraces, and reminisce on the old glories of the former palace in Amlapura. And for those more into watersports, Tulamben on the northeast coast offers a wide range of facilities.

Right: the east is a diving hotspot

9. Along the Northern Coast to Candi Dasa
(see map, p47)

Visit an artistic community, a waterfall and a salt-making village. Swim with tropical fish inhabiting a shipwreck in Tulamben and at a royal pleasure park. End at a coastal resort with an interesting temple complex.

This route can be done as a continuation of North Bali's Itinerary 8 after Pura Ponjok Batu rather than returning to Lovina. If you are already in Candi Dasa and on your way to the north, then do this in reverse to save time and avoid backtracking.

Drive along the north coast towards East Bali, stopping by at **Tejakula**. This coastal town has an old horse bath fed by a natural spring that was converted into a public bathing place. Cool water gushes out of spouts in separate male and female compartments.

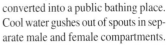

Artists in this area make colourful *wayang* (puppet figure) paintings and beautiful gold jewellery. Some of the best dancers and musical groups in Bali come from here, where the dynamic *kebyar* dance originated in the early 1900s. Rare *wayang wong* (masked drama) and group *baris* (warrior) dances are performed for temple ceremonies (see *pages 14–6*).

Found just 3km (1¾ miles) beyond Tejakula are some beautiful hills and a right turn-off into the mountains to **Les**. During the hot and rainy season (November–March) there is a beautiful waterfall for cooling off from the heat.

Further east, the landscape becomes dry and desolate; these were areas that were devastated during the 1963 eruption of Gunung Agung. You can still see blackened lava flows down the mountainside. Two villages along the way, **Tianyar** and **Kubu**, make salt the traditional way by evaporating seawater. Otherwise, there is not much else to see here, but it is an area of stark beauty where you witness the awesome power of nature.

Watersports & a Wreck

Just 5km (3 miles) after Kubu is **Tulamben**. Lying offshore is the wreck of the USS *Liberty* warship, which was torpedoed in January 1942 by a Japanese submarine in the Lombok Strait during World War II. It was towed to Tulamben but became filled with water and sank just before reaching shore.

Shockwaves from the 1963 volcanic eruption broke the wreck in half and caused it to move further away to its present underwater location. It is now home to a great variety of tropical fishes, and the clear waters are very good for diving around the wreck and other watersports. Equipment can be rented from hotels in the area, where you also can enjoy lunch.

Another 8km (5 miles) down the road is Culik. Take the left turn-off going 3 km (1¾ miles) east to **Amed**, another good watersports and diving

Above: extracting salt at Amed
Right: Taman Tirtha Gangga water spout detail

site with hotels that rent equipment. Villagers here also make their living by fishing and making salt.

Water of the Ganges

Return to Culik, turn left and drive 8km (5 miles) south, where startling changes in the arid landscape suddenly appear in the lush rice terraces between two picturesque hills in **Abang**. Continue just 2km (1¼ miles) more to **Taman Tirtha Gangga** (daily 8am–6pm; admission fee plus more for each pool).

Originally a holy water temple, this 'Ganges Water Garden' was built in 1948 by the last king of Karangasem. With its mixture of Balinese, Chinese and European architectural elements, the pleasure park was acclaimed as a marvel of engineering at the time.

It was a source of great pride to the king and his wives, who escaped from the heat and relaxed in royal pleasure in its landscaped gardens, open-air pavilions and cool pools. Although the structures suffered some damage during the 1963 eruption of Gunung Agung, most of the complex is still in fairly good condition.

The site is of extraordinary beauty with its lovely natural setting surrounded by hills and rice terraces. Fresh water flows out continuously from under a huge banyan tree into a series of large pools on different levels, gushing through a series of spouts and fountains.

Though usually fairly quiet during most of the day, except on weekends, the place comes alive in the late afternoons when locals flock to the pools

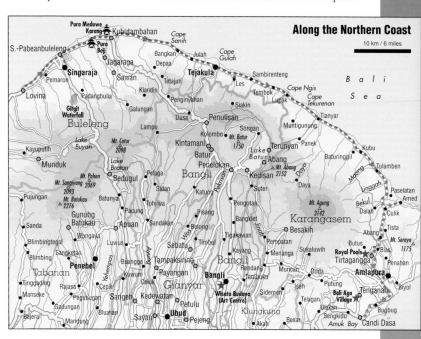

Along the Northern Coast

10 km / 6 miles

to bathe. There are toilets and changing rooms, so enjoy a refreshing swim followed by dinner at a restaurant in the complex. If you can't get enough, there are several good places for an overnight stay.

The Ten Temples

Otherwise, continue on to **Candi Dasa** with a wider range of facilities. The first bungalows appeared in the late 1970s near the white-sand beach, and their success led to a building boom in 1982.

Unfortunately, protective coral reefs were removed for construction materials. The waves came in and took the beach away. Ugly concrete piers jutting out into the water were built too late to be of any use. There hardly is a beach anymore, and oil pollution from passing tankers and a nearby petroleum storage facility make it even less inviting.

However, there are excellent beaches and interesting sights nearby. Giv-

ing its name to the area is **Pura Candi Dasa**, which, as its name suggests, is a series of 'Ten Temples' built on several levels on the hillside across from the spring-fed man-made lake. One of the upper temples within this 12th-century complex is the Hariti shrine, which originates from a legend about a child-eating ogress, who subsequently converted to Buddhism and became a protector of children. The Balinese call her Men Brayut, from the folktale of a mother who had 18 children. Women who want to conceive come to her to pray and make offerings.

Another flight of steep steps leads up to a Shiva temple with a *lingga* (phallic image) inside. The views are beautiful from here, especially with the colourful sails of outrigger fishing canoes dotting the sea.

Across the street from the temple is a man-made lagoon with lotuses. On the far ocean-side is the simple **Gandhi Ashram** (tel: 0363-4118), where the teachings and non-violent philosophy of the late Indian leader Mahatma Gandhi are promoted.

You can stay here in simple lodgings and meditate to the sound of waves at your doorstep. If you're lucky, you might meet the founder, Ibu Gedong Bagus Oka. She is one of Bali's most respected leaders. Gentle and unassuming, don't let her small size and age fool you, for she is very outspoken about issues pertaining to protecting the environment and culture from development. When she speaks, people listen.

For dinner, the **Pandan Restaurant** (tel: 0363-41541) by the beach or **TJ's** (tel: 0363-41540) at the Water Garden Hotel are pleasant places to eat.

Above: beach view at Candi Dasa

the east

10. TENGANAN AND AMLAPURA *(see map, p50)*

Visit a terraced village famous for its rare textiles and bloody ritual battles. Drop by the former palace and ruins of a royal pleasure park. Travel up to the mountains to see snakeskin fruit trees, then down through some old villages.

After an early breakfast, drive just to the west of Candi Dasa to a turn-off that goes about 4km (2½ miles) north to **Tenganan Pageringsingan**, or simply **Tenganan**, a Bali Aga (Aboriginal Balinese) village nestled in a lush valley with rich and well-cultivated land.

After entering a small gate, you'll see stone ramps on three lanes linking one broad terrace to the next. Ceremonial pavilions occupy the middle of the west lane, with walled house compounds of the purest descendants lining both sides. The east lane is for those who marry anyone from the outside.

Shimmering Cloths

Tenganan is the only place in Indonesia where the double-*ikat* cloth called *kain geringsing* is made. Villagers believe that Indra, the Hindu lord of storms created and taught the people of Tenganan how to weave these textiles.

Undyed threads for both weft and warp directions are wound on two separate frames that are the exact length and width of the finished cloth. Charcoal grids are marked on them, and waterproof fibres are tied in complex patterns. Then the threads are coloured with natural dyes. This may be repeated several times, with new sections tied off and others opened up. Finally, all the fibres are removed, and the threads are woven. The dyed sections overlap precisely to form exquisite designs. This extremely difficult and time-consuming technique is found only in a few villages in India and Japan.

Top: a young weaver at Tenganan
Right: wooden mask for offerings

Not every woman in Tenganan is patient or skilled enough to spend up to seven years making a single piece. Those who do strap themselves into small looms, leaning forward and back to adjust the tension of the threads with their bodies, nudging the threads into position with a pointed twig.

These cloths are believed to have protective properties and can cure illnesses. Its name may come from the words *gering* (ill) and *sing* (not), although *geringsing* itself means 'speckled', an appropriate description of these shimmering textiles.

Blood Rituals & Origins

Tenganan village is full of unusual customs and practices. During certain rituals, young women and men dressed in *geringsing* dance to the music of *gamelan selonding* (iron-keyed metallophones), an ancient version of the *gamelan*. During the annual Usaba Sambah (June–July) festival, young girls ride wooden ferris wheels propelled by foot power. In India, the Mahavrata festival for Indra has similar swinging rites symbolising the sun descending to unite with and give life to the earth. During Usaba Sambah, men fight the *makare*, using thorny leaves to ritually draw blood as sacrifice.

There is some evidence that the people of Tenganan originally came from the kingdom of Bedahulu (Bedulu). The legend of how they acquired their land dates back to the 14th century when King Bedahulu lost his horse and sent some villagers to search for it.

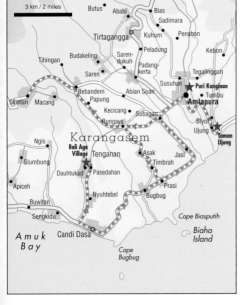

The men travelled east and found the body of the dead horse instead. When the king offered to reward them, they asked for the land where the horse was found, more precisely, wherever the dead horse could be smelt. The king's minister, who was sent to survey the land, walked over a wide area with the leader of the men, but could not escape the odour of the dead horse. When the tired minister finally left, the leader gleefully took out a hidden chunk of rotten horse meat from under his clothes. The villagers thus got extensive fields, which to this day are worked by tenant farmers in return for half the crop.

Above: the heart of rural Bali
Right: Amlapura sunset

Eclectic Royal Tastes

Drive back to the main road and stop for an early lunch in Candi Dasa (see *Eating Out, pages 75–9*). Continue 20km (12½ miles) east over the hills and into **Amlapura**. Follow the one-way streets all around the edge of town until you see **Puri Kanginan** (daily 9am–5pm; admission fee) on your left. Don't confuse this with the Puri Agung Karangasem which is located across the road and is much less interesting.

Enter the front courtyard of this 'Eastern Palace' to view the **Bale Kambang** set in the midst of a large pond. The royal family used this 'Floating Pavilion' for relaxation and entertainment. Nearby is the European-style **Bale Maskerdam**. Inside this 'Amsterdam Hall' are old photographs, sedan chairs and other royal artefacts. The tooth-filing pavilion has decorative features carved during the 1920s by Chinese craftsmen, a gift by the Chinese ruler to the king of Karangasem. In 1911, Heer van Kol in his *Goa Lawah to the Capitol*, was so struck by the Puri Kanginan that he described it thus:

'It was a large walled pavilion opening off a deep gallery, all very serene save for the rather startling interior decor. The doors were intricately carved and brightly painted and gilded in the Balinese manner, as were the windows and beams, but the furnishings were exclusively European. In the centre of the room stood a huge brass bedstead overhung by a richly-worked canopy and provided with silken counterpane, cushions and pillows. There were marble-top tables, carved and gilded chairs and mirrors, and hanging lamps with crystal pendants – all in the purest rococo, including an especially fanciful music box.'

From the centre of Amlapura near the market, look for the sign to the road that leads 4km (2½ miles) south to **Taman Ujung**. This picturesque pleasure park and ruins of a once-grand water palace of the last king of Karangasem was built in 1919 by Gusti Bagus Jelantik, and had a vast pool bordered by small pavilions and a European building with stained glass windows in the centre.

Most of it was destroyed by the 1963 volcanic eruption, and recent plans to restore it and turn it into an art centre with help from rock musician David Bowie fell through. The ruins are still worth a visit however.

Scenic Villages

Backtrack to Amlapura and head 2km (1¼ miles) west to Genteng, taking the small turn-off road leading 9km (5½ miles) uphill through Bebandem and over to **Sibetan**. The roadsides are lined with short and thorny palm trees that produce *salak*. If in season, buy this fruit with brown, scaly snake-like skin and crisp, sweet-tart flesh.

Return to Bebandem and take the road to your right going 8km (5 miles) downhill through the Bali Aga villages of **Bungaya**, **Asak** and **Timbrah**. Perpendicular to the main road are very narrow village lanes that allow only two people to pass. Long ceremonial pavilions are the focus of attention for Usaba Samba rituals held at the villages during June, July and August and featuring amazing towering offerings, ceremonial dances and battles, along with elaborately dressed young men and women who take part in the festivities.

The road joins the main coastal road, so turn right and head 6km (3¾ miles) west back over the hills to Candi Dasa. Along the way, pause to admire the scenery from a small pavilion along the roadside.

11. KLUNGKUNG, BESAKIH AND ON TO UBUD
(see map, p56)

Visit a bat cave and watch salt-makers. View painted ceilings, watch artists at work, and visit a temple in Klungkung. Travel to a mountain temple complex, then descend through stunning rice terraces and a village of weavers and bookmakers, ending at Ubud, the centre of 'cultural tourism' in Bali.

If you're already in the Ubud area, go via Klungkung, Kamasan, Gelgel, Besakih, Sidemen and Kusamba. From here, you can return to Ubud or move east on to Candi Dasa.

After breakfast, head west 21km (13 miles) along the coast to **Kusamba** to see villagers extracting salt using traditional methods. Wet sand is gathered from the sea and spread along the shore to dry. After drying, the sand is poured into large vats inside thatched huts, where the saline-rich water is left to drain. The residue is then poured into bamboo troughs and left to evaporate until salt crystals are formed.

Bats & Bullets

Drive 4km (2½ miles) east to **Pura Goa Lawah** and marvel at the thousands of bats amidst the pungent smell of their droppings covering the shrines. Sometimes, a python emerges from a roof crevice to devour an unsuspecting bat. They are all believed to be divine manifestations and thus protected. This 'Bat Cave Temple' is important for post-cremation rites.

Above: Puri Semarapura

the east

Legend has it that the cave leads all the way to Pura Besakih on Gunung Agung (see *page 55*). This was reputedly discovered when a Balinese prince who sought sanctuary in the bat cave found his way up to Besakih.

History also tells of Dutch forces camping nearby after defeating Buleleng and Jembrana in 1849. Dewa Agung Istri Kanya, the 'Virgin Queen' of Klungkung (see below), did not like having the enemy in her territory, so using a special gun, she fired a magical bullet made of metal and the internal organs of a sacrificed man. The bullet flew a great distance and entered the thigh of the Dutch commander. From there, it travelled through his body, seeking and destroying the same organs it was made from. Miraculously, it then emerged from the dead man and flew back on its own volition to Klungkung for purification and future re-use against enemies.

Palace & Paintings

Like the bullet, head 13km (8 miles) to **Klungkung**, the last royal capital. In 1908, the royal family committed suicide in a *puputan* (sacrifice), their sacred weapons defiled and rendered useless by holy water purposely contaminated with urine by the Dutch. Most of **Puri Semarapura** (daily 9am–5pm; admission fee), the 'Fortress of Love Palace', was destroyed, but **Bale Kerta Gosa** still stands. In this 'Consultation Pavilion for Peace and Prosperity', the king sat on a chair with lions (symbolic of the ruler) carved on its arms, while three high priests sat in chairs carved with holy cow heads. A secretary and a Dutch official sat on serpent-armed chairs. Statues of Balinese, Europeans and Chinese stand nearby.

The amazing ceiling murals in the puppet style of Kamasan, repainted on asbestos panels several times since the 1920s, illustrate the *Bima Swarga* story from the Indian *Mahabharata* epic. The hero, Bima, goes to the Buddhist underworld and fights demons and the god of hell to recover the souls of his father and stepmother.

Bale Kambang rests nearby on a giant stone turtle that seems to float in the middle of a pond, thus giving the pavilion its name. The royal family would while their time

Above: Kamasan ceiling murals, Bale Kerta Gosa
Right: statue at Puri Semarapura

away in pleasure while being entertained here. Cross the causeway lined with mythological figures and the occasional Dutchman. The ceiling is painted with the story of Prince Sutasoma, the hero, and his adventures in defeating a man-eating demon who then converts to Buddhism, the Buddhist *Brayut* folktale of a couple named Pan and Men Brayut with 18 children, and the 35 Balinese astrological signs.

Memorials & Monuments

Further back is the *kori agung* (main gate) of the palace. Look for Chinese, Portuguese and Dutch figures on it alongside demons and animals. The wooden doors, carved with monkey brothers Sugriva and Vali from the Hindu *Ramayana* epic, were said to have shut by themselves after the *puputan* massacre in 1908, and no-one has been able or even dared to open them.

A large building nearby has displays of artefacts, photographs, dance costumes and textiles from Klungkung. Another section has paintings and sculptures by the late Italian artist, Emilio Ambron, who once lived in Bali and donated his works to the local government.

Across the street is the towering black **Monumen Puputan Klungkung** that commemorates the *puputan* or suicide-massacre of the royal family. In the hollow base are statues and dioramas depicting the rise and fall of the last Balinese kingdom.

The main intersection is guarded by the **Kanda Pat**, a modern shrine dedicated to the 'Four Siblings' that emerge at birth: clear amniotic fluid, red blood, yellow *vernix caseosa* (waxy substance on the skin) and dark placenta. Figures of four Hindu gods face each direction and are dressed in their appropriate cosmic colours that also symbolise the Kanda Pat: Ishvara (faces east, in white), Brahma (faces south, in red), Mahadeva (faces west, in yellow) and Vishnu (faces north, in black).

Head south from the statues 3km (1¾ miles), then at the crossroads turn left to go 1km (½ mile) to **Gelgel**, known for its beautiful hand-woven cloths, for a look at **Pura Dasar**.

11. klungkung, besakih and on to ubud

Members of the *pasek* clans worship at this 'Foundation Temple' with its multi-roofed *meru* (pagodas) during its festival (see *Calendar of Events, pages 83–5*). Look for simple stone seats outside under a banyan tree, remnants of Bali's megalithic past.

Drive a short distance north to **Kamasan** to see painters making *wayang-* (puppet-) style works. Artists here still use bamboo brushes and natural pigments. You may stay and watch the complete process done by Nyoman Arcana and others in Banjar Sangging and Pande Mas. Craftsmen here also make beautiful metal bowls for offerings. Some of them even carve intricate designs onto used artillery cases, giving new life to these instruments of death.

The 'Mother Temple'

Drive west through the village and out to the main road, turn right to go north pass the marketplace and bus terminal, and back to Klungkung. From the main crossroads, go north 21km (13 miles) to **Pura Besakih**, the largest temple complex on the island, and which traces its origins to the 8th century.

Besakih began as an ancient terraced sanctuary for worshipping the god of the volcano, **Gunung Agung**, dominating the landscape at 3,142m (10,300ft). Over a period of 1,000 years, the complex was enlarged to its present size of about 30 temples and hundreds of shrines. It was the state temple of the Gelgel and Klungkung kingdoms.

In February 1963, during preparations for the Ekadasa Rudra sacrifice held once a century, glowing clouds of ash belched from Gunung Agung. In March, the volcano erupted violently, having been dormant since 1843, killing thousands and destroying many temples and villages. Built on a ridge, however, Pura Besakih was spared.

Most Balinese viewed the eruption as punishment for performing the ritual at the wrong time, while others saw it as a supernatural presence that needed to be appeased with human victims. In 1979, a properly-timed Ekadasa Rudra ceremony was held without incident.

The most important temple here is **Pura Penataran Agung Besakih** with its many multi-roofed *meru* (pagodas). Only worshippers may enter, but visitors can circle the outer walls to glimpse inside and for spectacular views beyond (check out the view from the northeastern end).

Left: the 'Mother Temple' of Besakih
Top: offerings at a demon statue **Right:** Balinese Hindus in ceremonial garb

Inside the main courtyard are three seats for the three forms of Shiva, the destroyer. Two other temples together symbolise the Hindu trinity: **Pura Kiduling Kreteg** (Temple South of the Bridge) below for Brahma, the creator, and **Pura Batu Madeg** (Temple of the Upright Stone) above for Vishnu, the preserver.

There are several small restaurants in the parking lot with mediocre food, so take a break for lunch. Return to the main road and drive south 2km (1¼ miles) to Rendang, turning left on a road leading 4km (2½ miles) east to the old-fashioned village of **Muncan**, where mountainsides along the way are carved into spectacular rice terraces.

Continue 6km (3¾ miles) east through Selat to Duda, turning right and down south 10km (6¼ miles) to the rural and scenic **Sidemen**, famous for its beautiful hand-woven textiles, particularly the *songket*, and the illustrated *lontar* (inscribed palm-leaf books).

Continue downhill 6km (3¾ miles) until the junction at the main road, turn right and backtrack past Klungkung for 9km (5½ miles) until you see a big symbol for the region on the right side of a picturesque bend in the road. Stop nearby on the left side to dine on tasty Balinese-style grilled fresh fish at **Bali Languan** restaurant. From here, it's an easy drive to Gianyar and on to Ubud via Bedulu (Bedahulu).

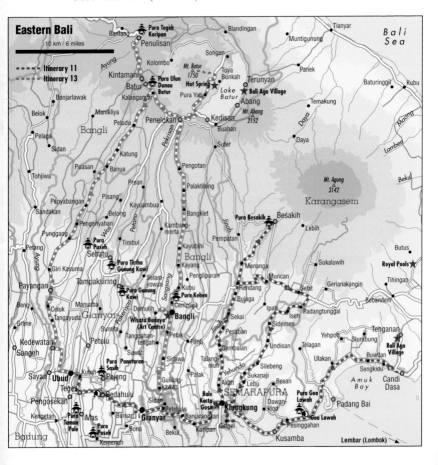

the Centre & Southeast

A series of rivers radiate out in all directions from the crater-lake of Gunung Batur, cutting deep valleys and irrigating fertile rice fields in Central Bali all the way down to the coast. These were ideal places for establishing the oldest kingdoms on the island, as areas around Kintamani, Pejeng and Bedulu prove, with temples and relics from the 9th-century Warmadewa dynasty.

During the late 11th century, the Balinese Buddhist King Udayana married the Javanese Hindu Princess Mahendradatta. This marriage created a political union of the two islands, with the larger Java dominating, and led to a fusion of the two religions into a Shiva-Buddha cult, incorporating animistic beliefs, indigenous ancestor worship and magical practices.

The couple had many children, but the two most important in history were Airlangga (Erlangga), who ruled on Java, and his younger brother Anak Wungsu, who became king of Bali.

The region, however, faded from history with the Javanese conquest in the 14th century. Puppet rulers were put into power, but as Islam spread in Java, Hindu-Buddhists sought refuge in Gelgel, which had become an independent Balinese kingdom.

Internal strife during the late 17th century led to civil war, eventually resulting in the founding of Klungkung. Princes from this royal family also set up other courts in Sukawati and Bangli during the mid-18th century.

When the rogue kingdom of Gianyar rose soon after, most of Central Bali became embroiled in wars that lasted until the late 19th century. The Dutch came in, and Klungkung finally succumbed to them in 1908.

Rich in history and culture, the region of Gianyar was the focus for the island's tourism during the 1920s, a trend that continues today. Ubud is one of the main tourist centres and accessible from all parts of the island. It offers a wide range of lodgings and has some of Bali's best restaurants. It is also an ideal base for visiting ancient temples and seeing beautiful countryside. Nearby Sayan is where exciting whitewater rafting trips on the Ayung River begin.

The central areas offer many opportunities to learn about Balinese culture. Dance performances are held every night in and around Ubud, while arts and crafts are home industries in many villages.

Right: topeng masked dancer in Ubud

12. UBUD'S HIGHLIGHTS *(see map, p58)*

Start with a visit to the market and art museum, followed by a ridge walk down to a temple. View another museum collection, then explore a monkey forest and surrounding areas.

If the weather is clear, put on a good walking shoes and dress comfortably.

After an early breakfast, go to the *pasar* (marketplace) in the centre of **Ubud** to see the variety of items available for sale. On every third day, called *pasah* (check a printed Balinese calendar), the market area overflows with sellers and buyers. However, wait until another time to buy so that you don't have to carry your purchases on this tour.

Across the street, peer in at the front courtyard of **Puri Saren**, the residence of Ubud's royal family. From the main crossroads head west (or hop into one of the waiting public minivans), following the road as it turns north. After 1km (½ mile) is the **Museum Neka** (daily 9am–5pm; admission fee), founded in 1976 by Suteja Neka, a schoolteacher-turned-art collector.

A series of buildings amidst beautiful gardens houses an excellent collection showing the different styles of Balinese painting through history. Works by foreign artists, especially Arie Smit, are a highlight, as are photographs from the 1930s. Every piece has an informative label, so allow time (at least 2 hours) to learn more about Balinese art and culture. Afterwards, relax and enjoy the view at the museum's open-air snack shop.

A Priestly Path

Go 1km (½ mile) north by foot or public minivan up the main road towards **Kedewatan**, famous for fuzzy red *rambutan* or *buluan*. Buy some of these sweet fruits if they are in season, along with bottled water to take with you on the ridge walk.

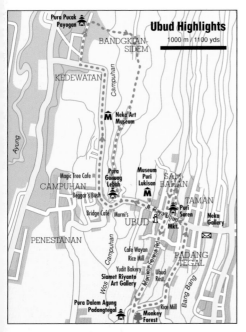

Follow the sign to **Pura Pucak Payogan**, the 'Summit Temple of Meditation', where during the 8th century, the holy man Resi Markandeya meditated after coming from Java, having followed a bright light to Bali. Just to the right, a narrow paved road winds down a river valley and up the other side to **Bangkiansidem** (Ant's Waist), named because this village lies on a narrow ridge between two broader sections.

The road ends at a paved footpath, so if you hire a driver with a car, have him wait at the staircase near the eastern end of the bridge in Campuhan. Continue on the path for a leisurely 1-km (½-mile) stroll with magnificent vistas of the coun-

the centre & southeast

tryside spreading out before you. The hillsides are covered with *lalang* or *ambengan*, the grass used for thatching. Down below, you may be able to see people cutting out blocks of *paras* rock from the riverbanks. This compressed ash and clay is mostly used for carving statues and building temples.

On a clear day, you can see Gunung Agung rising majestically in the east on your left, the source of the light that Resi Markandeya followed. Look back at the view of palm trees and mountains. Continue down the path and pass by a small, unfinished house known as *rumah hantu* (haunted house).

The walk ends at **Pura Gunung Lebah**, the 'Temple of the Low Mountain' or Gunung Batur, dedicated to the lake goddess of Danau Batur. It was renovated in the early 1990s. Resi Markandeya built his home at this holy site where two rivers meet, **Campuhan** (confluence).

The Balinese hold purification rituals here. You can go down to the river to cool off, but be careful because the current can be swift and the river is deep especially during the rainy season (November–March).

Tripping Around Town

From the river, take the staircase up to the bridge (where your driver will be waiting if you've hired one). Stop for lunch at one of the restaurants along the main road leading back into Ubud (see *Eating Out, pages 75–9*).

Next, drop by **Museum Puri Lukisan** (daily 8am–4pm; admission), set in attractive gardens. Founded in 1956, it features works by Balinese painters and carvers of the Pitamaha (Noble Aspiration), a famous artists' association active from 1936–42 in Ubud.

Return east to the main crossroads and turn left for a 1-km (½-mile) walk south along Jalan Wanara Wana (Monkey Forest Road) to a small **Monkey Forest**. The animals can be aggressive, so hang on to your belongings. Nearby is **Pura Dalem Agung**

Above: palatial trimmings at Puri Saren
Right: Ubud market

Padangtegal, the great temple of the dead with an ornately-carved gate.

Continue east along the road until it meets up with Jalan Hanoman, then turn left for another 1-km (½-mile) walk north back to the main road in Ubud. If you have time, head west until you come to a small road on your right before the marketplace. Turn up this road, which does a short 1-km (½-mile) north-west-south loop through quiet **Sambahan** back to the centre of town.

Return to your hotel and relax before attending an early evening dance performance (see *pages 14–6 and 97*). Dinner options in Ubud are plentiful (see *Eating Out, pages 75–9*) but always popular is **Café Wayan** on Monkey Forest Road. Run by Ibu Wayan and her family, the fusion fare and cakes served here are delicious.

13. NORTH TO BATUR AND KINTAMANI *(see map, p56)*

Journey up into the mountains and climb an active volcano if you wish, or just relax in the hot springs. After lunch, stop by two temples on the crater rim and visit another built on terraces.

If you plan to climb the volcano, leave as early as possible to avoid the midday heat, and wear good walking shoes and dress comfortably. Don't attempt this during the rainy season (November–March), as it can get dangerously slippery on the sandy slopes.

Get onto the road north out of Ubud through Payangan and drive 32km (20 miles) all the way up to **Kintamani**. Turn right and drive along the scenic crater rim road for 3km (1¾ miles) to **Penelokan**, which means 'viewpoint' because of the stunning vista of active volcano and crater-lake below.

The crater is 14km (8¾ miles) across at its widest diameter, and in the middle stands the black cone of **Gunung Batur** (1,717m/5,635ft), an active volcano that lets out occasional puffs of ash. The last minor eruption was in 1994, although nothing major has occurred since 1926. At its foot is **Danau Batur**, the largest lake on the island. Its depth has never been recorded, but it is the source for most of the rivers in the eastern half of Bali.

This amazing natural setting epitomises the Balinese concept of *rwa bhineda* (complementary opposites) with fire (volcano) and water (lake), much like the Chinese *yin-yang* philosophy. Don't let the aggressive vendors disturb you; consider it another manifestation of complementary opposites.

Descend 8km (5 miles) into the crater down a winding road through lava fields to **Toya Bungkah**, where there is an art centre. Climb the volcano from here along well-marked trails, or if in doubt, hire a guide from a nearby hotel (see *Practical Information, page 95*). It takes around 4–5 hours for the trek but the surface is rather loose and sandy, so be careful.

Whether you climb or not, take a relaxing soak in the *yeh panes* (natural hot springs) here. Don't jump right in, as the water can be close to scalding hot. Start at the tepid end near the lake and move up gradually to the

Above: temple detail from Pura Dalem Agung Padangtegal
Top Right: Gunung Batur **Right:** the hot springs of Toya Bungkah

hotter source. Afterwards, have lunch at a nearby restaurant – **Nyoman Mawa** by the lake has excellent fried fish served with raw chilli-onion relish – or up on the rim at **Kintamani Restaurant** which serves buffet-style meals to busloads of tourists.

Childless Chinese

Back on the rim, drive 4km (2½ miles) north to **Pura Ulun Danu Batur**, Bali's second most important temple complex. It was relocated here in 1926 when lava flows destroyed the original one at the edge of the lake below. The largest temple, **Pura Penataran Agung Batur**, is dedicated to the lake goddess.

The gates are towering architectural masterpieces, and there is an air of mystery in the late afternoon when mists roll in. Inside the temple is a Chinese shrine dedicated to Ida Ratu Ayu Subandar, the Harbour Mistress, where merchants, traders and business people come to pray for success during the temple's festival (see *Calendar of Events, pages 83–5*).

Legend tells of Bali's 11th-century King Mayadanawa, who married a Chinese princess and converted to Buddhism. He took on another title reflecting the union, Balingkang ('Bali' plus 'Kang', her Chinese family name). However, the Hindu gods did not approve and cursed her to be *mandul* (childless). When she died of sorrow, the king built the shrine in her memory.

The king subsequently went to war against the Hindu gods but was killed. The legend of Mayadanawa's defeat in battle is remembered every 210 days during the Galungan holiday (see *Calendar of Events, pages 83–5*). The legend is also a metaphor of the decline of Buddhism and the rise of Hinduism in Bali, although in reality the two faiths are fused together.

Drive a further 3km (1¾ miles) uphill to **Pura Tegeh Koripan** (also known as **Pura Puncak Penulisan**, named after the nearby peak) and climb the long

staircase to this ancient 'High Life Temple' enshrouded by mists. On clear days, the views are spectacular. Gazing about silently from pavilions and shrines are dozens of statues of ancient deified kings and queens, carved between the 10th and 14th century, including one of the childless Chinese princess, Bhatari Mandul.

Terraced Temple

Backtrack along the rim road and take the turn-off south at Penelokan down to Bangli. If you have time, after 16km (10 miles), take a right turn-off in Kubu and go west to **Penglipuran**, a village built on terraces. All the houses are built in the same way with gateways in one matching style. It's monotonous, contrary to the meaning of its name, 'Entertainment'.

Continue on to **Bangli**, and just north of town, take a winding road going to the right for 1km (½ mile) west to **Bukit Demulih**. This is the 'Hill of No Return' because its beautiful views will make you not want to go home. However, do go back to the main road and head east to **Pura Kehen**. Built during the 11th century on terraces under a huge banyan tree, this temple has dozens of shrines and an 11-tiered *meru* (pagoda) dedicated to Shiva. Festivals here have processions of beautiful offerings and ceremonial warrior dances (see *Calendar of Events, pages 83–5*).

Return to the main road and go 7km (4¼ miles) south to **Sidan**, where just before the turn to the east is the **Pura Dalem**, which has a beautifully-carved temple gate. The road turns south again and soon meets up at a major junction. Turn right and travel 2km (1¼ miles) west to **Gianyar**.

By late afternoon, the streets next to the town's market will be lined with vendor stalls for the night fair. Browse around with the locals and try some of the food such as roast suckling pig, fried fish with hot sauce, smoked chicken and Balinese sweets, or head back to Ubud via Bedulu (Bedahulu) for more hygienic restaurant fare (see *Eating Out, pages 75–9*).

the centre & southeast

14. BEDULU, TAMPAKSIRING AND TEGALALANG
(see map, p64)

Enter the mouth of a monster and visit two temple complexes. Marvel at towering funerary monuments and some water temples. View amazing rice terraces, and watch thousands of herons roosting at sunset.

Have an early breakfast and pack along a lunch or snack, then head south out of Ubud through Peliatan. Follow the main road as it turns east for 2km (1¼ miles) to **Bedulu** (or Bedahulu) to **Goa Gajah**. Descend the steps to the 'Elephant Cave', which dates from the 11th century and is carved out of solid rock. The huge monstrous face is supposed to frighten away evil, a motif usually seen above temple gates called Bhoma, a Hindu fertility figure. The other surfaces are covered with figures of people, animals and demons amidst stylised scenery.

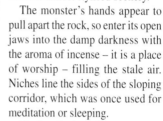

The monster's hands appear to pull apart the rock, so enter its open jaws into the damp darkness with the aroma of incense – it is a place of worship – filling the stale air. Niches line the sides of the sloping corridor, which was once used for meditation or sleeping.

The interior has a T-shape. At the left (west) end is a four-armed stone image of Ganesha, elephant-headed Hindu lord of obstacles, giving the name to the cave. At the right (east) end are three *lingga* (phallic images of Shiva, Hindu god of destruction and reincarnation) with eight smaller ones around each, all on a common base and carved from a single stone. While these images are Hindu, the cave was also once a Buddhist sanctuary.

In front of the cave is a bathing place with steps leading down to male and female sections. The place is no longer used for bathing, however. Water pours out of jars held by six voluptuous female stone figures, whose upper halves once stood outside the cave entrance.

In 1954, a Dutch archaeologist, using information from villagers, excavated the area and uncovered the matching lower halves of the statues. Behind this is **Pura Taman**, a temple with a shrine in the middle of a pond. South of the bathing place are steps leading down to a river. Cross the bridge and nearby are the remains of a relief carving of Buddhist temple structures.

Meetings & Measurements

Return up to the main road and continue east for 1km (½ mile) beyond the intersection to **Pura Samuan Tiga**. This huge 'Tripartite Meeting Temple' is the third most important in Bali and was the state temple of the War-madewa dynasty which ruled up to the 14th century. The name may refer to the blend of animism, Buddhism and Hinduism practised in Bali today.

Top Left: statue at Pura Dalem in Sidan
Left: offerings at Pura Kehen **Above:** the mystical Goa Gajah cave

Built on a series of terraces, there are dozens of shrines, some housing ancient stone figures of deities and phallic images. The temple has undergone continuous renovation since 1994 but still retains an atmosphere of awe and power. Festivals here have huge processions, ritual dances and mock battles (see *Calendar of Events, pages 83–5*).

Under a huge banyan tree are three multi-tiered brick-and-stone *meru* (pagodas), structures usually made of wood and thatching found in most Balinese temples. From north to south (left to right), these are dedicated to the deities of the lakes, wealth and sea, representing the upper, middle and lower realms of the spiritual world. People usually pray here for material success.

Some pavilions house ancient sculptures of goddess of death – Durga trampling the buffalo demon, phallic representations of god of destruction Shiva, and other Hindu deities. The main gate leading to the terraces has a face of Bhoma, a Hindu fertility figure who frightens away evil. The highest terrace has curious shrines found nowhere else in Bali.

Continue on the narrow road going east past the temple and follow it north for 4km (2½ miles) through Petemon and Sawagunung all the way up to the 12th-century temple complex of **Pura Penguku-rukuran**. Rich carvings adorn the walls and gates of this 'Temple of Measurements'.

Above: Pura Gunung Kawi

Walk carefully down a steep flight of enormous stone steps to the river, a quiet place with an air of mystery and a good place to eat and cool off. There are three small niches nearby, one with some statues. Examine the arrangement carefully, for villagers say that if you look again later, the figures may have shifted places by themselves.

A small path downstream leads you up to the main road. Backtrack 2km (1¼ miles) south and turn right at a junction that takes you the same distance west. The road emerges at the main intersection in Pejeng.

A Royal Memorial

From here, turn right and continue north for 13km (8 miles) uphill to **Tampaksiring** until you see a sign on your right for **Pura Gunung Kawi**. Descend a long and steep flight of steps into a picturesque river valley and gaze in wonder at the towering façades of the 11th-century temple complex carved out of solid rock and overlooking the river.

This 'Mountain Temple of Poets' is a memorial to King Anak Wungsu of the Warmadewa dynasty. They are not tombs, for no ashes of cremated bodies were deposited here. The 7-m (23-ft) high carvings resemble 9th-century Javanese *candi* (memorial shrines).

A cluster of four *candi* on the west bank are monuments to the king's minor consorts, while five more across the river are for the king, queen and important family members. Water flows through small channels and pours out from spouts into a pool that once served as a royal bath.

Located nearby is a cluster of niches and enclosed rooms, also cut from solid rock, that may have once been a Buddhist monastery (so please remove your footwear before entering). An adjoining temple in the more typical style provides a striking contrast in architecture.

Water, Water Everywhere

Return to the main road and continue 1km (½ mile) north to a crossroads and turn right. A sign on your right indicates a road to **Pura Mengening**, a small 'Clear Water Temple' with a holy spring under a banyan tree. Nearby is a larger newly-renovated temple with a restored ancient building inside resembling the temple façades at Pura Gunung Kawi.

Backtrack to the main road and continue to nearby **Pura Tirtha Empul**, a 10th-century temple with holy water gushing out from many spouts, each with a different ritual use. Their common source is a spring that bubbles up through the ground of an enclosed pool inside the temple.

Legend tells of the ferocious Buddhist King Mayadanawa who fought against Indra, the Hindu god of storms. Mayadanawa created a pond that poisoned the gods when they drank from it. But by hurling a thunderbolt into the ground, Indra caused the antidote to spring up, thus giving

Right: in the festive mood

the centre & southeast

this 'Temple of Bubbling Elixir' its name. On high ground above the temple is a huge residence built by the late Sukarno, Indonesia's first president. It is closed to the public, but the view of the temple below is lovely. From here, Sukarno supposedly spied on bathing beauties below, but the public baths have since been moved from sight.

Return to the main Tampaksiring road and drive across to a winding road that goes for 2km (1¼ miles) to another water temple in Sebatu, **Pura Tirtha Gunung Kawi**, dedicated to the lake goddess of Danau Batur. The pavilions and shrines are covered with colourful carvings.

Adjacent to the temple are separate male and female bathing sections. The carved spouts are fed by water cascading down from a lush fern-covered hillside and into a fish pond with a shrine in the middle.

Spectacular Sights

Follow the road uphill for 2km (1¼ miles) and turn left to head south to Pujung along the main road, stopping after 3km (1¾ miles) at **Kampung Café** in Ceking to eat and take in the dramatic view of rice terraces. Continue south for the same distance to get a closer look at this spectacular sculpted landscape in **Tegalalang**, where villagers also make woodcarvings.

Before sunset, head 7km (4¼ miles) down the road and take a right turn-off marked by a sign to **Petulu**. Around this time, thousands of *kokokan* (white herons) will be returning to roost in the trees. Watch from a safe distance to avoid the rain of bird droppings. Legend says that the gods sent the birds as a sign for villagers to stop their revenge killings following the 1965 attempted communist coup in Jakarta. In reality, the herons left their forest home when it was cleared for a new road.

Before dark, continue 2km (1¼ mile) north up the road and turn left at the junction south to **Junjungan** and **Kutuh** for glimpses of rural life. The road emerges after 5km (3 miles) in Ubud. Spend the evening at a performance or just relax over dinner (see *Eating Out, pages 75–9*).

15. GIANYAR'S ANCIENT SITES *(see map, p64)*

See the world's largest kettledrum and some erotic temple sculptures. Visit an archaeological museum and see dramatic relief carvings. Climb up to a hilltop shrine, watch musical instruments being made, and visit a Chinese temple. Drop by another ancient site, and enjoy dinner overlooking a scenic river valley.

Have an early breakfast and pack along lunch or snacks. Drive all the way to the east end of the main road in Ubud and cross the intersection to a small paved road that winds down a river valley and up the other side. At the junction in Sala, turn right and zigzag 2km (1¼ mile) through scenic rice fields

to Tatiapi where **Pura Agung Batan Bingin** is located.

Admire the carvings on this temple's outer walls depicting scenes from the Hindu *Ramayana* epic. Inside are many shrines with beautiful sculpted details. Many trees grow in this 'Great Temple Under The Banyan', and other temples make up this lovely complex.

The Bronze Moon

Continue for 1km (½ mile) east to the main crossroads in **Pejeng**, then turn right and go south to **Pura Penataran Sasih** (State Temple of the Moon). Amid an assortment of ancient stone figures is the largest bronze kettledrum gong in the world, known as the 'Moon of Pejeng'. It has a 160-cm (63-inch) diameter head and a height of 187cm (73 inches).

Lying on its side high up in a pavilion, this gong may have been cast as early as 300 BC. Look up at the eight eyes forming a central star surrounded by wavy lines. On the sides, faces stare out with wide-open eyes, their pierced earlobes stretched by heavy rings. Notice that a piece of the base is missing. The story goes that one night, one of the 13 moons (or a wheel from the moon's chariot) fell from the sky and landed in a tree. A thief came upon it and urinated on it to extinguish the glow. The moon exploded and killed him, then fell to the ground and cracked. The kettledrum is the *sasih* (moon) and is venerated by villagers, although it is never sounded, even during its festival (see *Calendar of Events, pages 83–5*).

Ancient Erotic Art

Continue a short distance south down the main road to **Pura Pusering Jagat**, a large temple famous for its very realistic stone *lingga* (phallic image) and *yoni* (vagina). Childless couples come here to pray for children.

Nearby is a large cylindrical stone vessel. Its sides are carved with images of gods and demons searching for the elixir of life in a scene from the *Mahabharata* epic. A nearby depression in the ground is the navel of this 'Tem-

Left: farmer in Tegalalang against sculpted rice terraces
Above: Pura Penataran Sasih

ple of the Navel of the Universe'. Offerings placed here vanish and allegedly re-appear far away at Pura Dalem Peed (pronounced 'puh-aid') on Nusa Penida off the southeast coast (see *page 31*).

Just down the road is **Pura Kebo Edan**. This 'Temple of the Crazy Buffalo' is famous for its large 14th-century statue of a masked giant with serpent-entwined legs dancing on a demon. His equally giant penis adorned with stimulating knobs swings to the left, symbolic of the Tantric ritual indulgence of forbidden acts.

Keep going south a short distance to **Museum Purbakala Gedong Arca** (Tues–Sun 8.30am–2pm; admission fee), a small archaeological museum with displays of ancient artefacts. The most fascinating are large stone sarcophagi with curious protruding heads on the upper and lower halves, looking like mating turtles. These prehistoric coffins show that prehistoric Balinese buried their dead before Buddhists and Hindus introduced cremation.

Dramas in Stone

Continue south 3km (1¾ miles) into **Bedulu** (Bedahulu), crossing the bend in the main road. At the end of the road, walk on a paved path through rice fields to **Yeh Pulu**. Large narrative relief carvings adorn a rock wall, showing life during the 14th century, believed to have been carved by legendary Balinese strongman Kebo Iwa using his fingernails.

In the series of images, a man is carrying pots of water, a woman peers out from her house, a horseback rider watches a hunt of wild boars, and a woman grabs the tail of his steed. These may be scenes of Krishna's youth, although such stories of the Hindu god were not known in Bali.

Backtrack all the way to the bend in the main road and turn right, heading 2km (1¾ miles) east to Semabaung. Turn right again at the traffic light to go to nearby Kutri to a cluster of three temples: **Pura Puseh**, **Pura Bukit Dharma**, and **Pura Kedharman**.

Climb the steps up a small hill to see a dramatic statue of Hindu goddess Durga, with multiple arms holding all sorts of weapons, slaying a buffalo demon. Although faceless, the figure may represent Mahendradatta, the infamous 11th-century Javanese queen who used black magic to kill her Balinese husband and became the widow-witch Rangda of exorcist drama (see *History & Culture, page 14*).

Sounds of Music & Mystery

Drive some 4km (2½ miles) south on the main road to **Blahbatuh**, turning left at Banjar Antugan to see the foundry of **Pande Made Gableran**. Watch melted bronze being poured into moulds, workers noisily hammering out gongs for *gamelan* musical instruments, and carvers making wooden cases.

Back on the main road, continue south past an orchid nursery and turn left at the junction to **Pura Gaduh**. Don't miss the humorous figures flanking the towering gate inside of women making love to horses. A pavilion houses a large and fearsome stone head of Kebo Iwa, the

Left: Yeh Pulu priestess

gigantic strongman who carved the Yeh Pulu reliefs with his bare hands.

Return to the junction and head west until you come to a bridge. Just below it is **Wihara Amurwabhumi**, a Chinese Buddhist temple overlooking a river gorge. People believe that if mysterious shouts are heard coming from down below on holy nights, an accident will happen on the bridge.

Temples Old & New

Back on the main road, continue 3km (1¾ miles) west to **Blahtanah**. If you have time, along the way is **Gapura Canggi** on your left. Follow the turn south to see an unusual gate and sculptures that date from the 14th century. A more recent temple was built in the same complex, providing a striking architectural contrast.

At the busy junction in **Sakah** leading to Mas and Ubud is a huge and grotesque statue of **Brahmarare**, the Hindu god of creation Brahma, as a baby. Follow the sign across the junction for a short drive to **Pura Hyang Tiba** with its great gates. This 'Temple of Divine Descent' was mentioned in an 11th-century inscription, although a stone carving of a moon, eye, elephant and bow, is a coded date for Saka year 1285 or AD 1363.

Go back to the main road and turn right for a 2-km (1¼-mile) drive south to **Batuan**, turning right again near a big demon statue. If you have time, stop and admire the intricately-carved outer walls of **Pura Desa**.

Continue west for 1km (½ mile), then turn left and drive the same distance south. A right turn-off going 2km (1¼ miles) west leads through **Singapadu**. If time permits, see **Pura Puseh** with its beautifully-carved shrines.

Turn right at the junction and go uphill 13km (8 miles) north to Sayan and **Kedewatan**, where you can enjoy dinner with stunning sunset views of the river valley below at a restaurant in one of the area's resort hotels (see *Practical Information, pages 91–6*). The **Amandari** hotel in Sayan is exquisite but expensive and the dress code here is smart, but if you prefer a more casual setting, the **Cahaya Dewata** hotel on the Sayan ridge offers just as wonderful views of the gorge.

Above: Yeh Pulu carvings

Leisure Activities

SHOPPING

The Balinese are renowned for their artistic skills, and you will find lots of souvenirs to cart back home. As the range of local crafts, art, antiques, jewellery and clothes is so huge, it takes a bit of hunting and rummaging to find what's right for you. Be prepared for the hard-sell sales pitch of some shopkeepers; the pressure to buy can be great. In shops without 'Fixed Price' signs, bargaining is necessary. Start at one-third of the asking price, and the vendor will lower his price as you raise yours. Stop at the amount you really want to spend – about one-half to two-thirds of the asking price. If the seller refuses, just walk away; you'll probably be called back to buy at your last bid. There is no better place to hone your bargaining skills than in the shops of Bali. Treat it as a game, and you will enjoy your purchases all the more.

Most shops are open daily from 9am to 9pm, but morning hours are best for bargaining. If accompanied by a guide or driver, prices may go up by 30 percent to include his commission. If alone, your bargaining power may be limited by unfamiliarity with the language and culture. The choice is yours. Below are some shopping recommendations. Note: Jl (Jalan) means 'Street'.

Antiques

It is illegal to take items which are over 50-years-old out of Indonesia, so it is unlikely that you will find real antique pieces. Be careful, as many 'new antiques' are intentionally weathered and ravaged to look old. Antique ceramics, textiles, carvings, puppets and jewellery from Bali and elsewhere in Indonesia can be found.

The most reliable place for genuine antiques is Denpasar's **Arts of Asia**, at Jl Thamrin Block C 27–37, (tel: 233350). **Mega Art Shop**, at Jl Gajah Mada 36–38, (tel: 224592), also in Denpasar, has a good range of antique and art items at reasonable prices.

The north end of Jl Tanjung Sari in Sanur has a number of antique shops. In Kuta, try **Eddy's**, along Jl Raya Basangkasa (tel: 730510); **Mayang Bali**, at Kuta Square Block A-12 (tel: 752902); **Pelack**, at Jl Bypass Ngurah Rai 9X (tel: 720244); and **Wijaya**, along Jl Legian Kelod (tel: 754011).

The road through Batubulan has shops like **Puri Sakana** (tel: 298205, 298210), and continues up to Batuan with **Jati** (tel: 298442). In Ubud, visit **Shalimar** (tel: 977115), at Jl Raya Ubud, near the market. In Klungkung, some shops in the town centre also trade in antiques.

Indonesian Crafts

Vendors from all over Indonesia sell their wares in Bali. Some products, like Sumba blankets, Asmat carvings and Javanese statues, are even made in Bali. Crafts from Lombok are sold in roadside shops in Sukawati and Peliatan. Also try **Matra'I**, along Jl Legian Kelod (tel: 240521) and **Pertokoan Citra Bali**, Jimbaran (tel: 702356).

Look for beautiful pots at **Lombok Pottery Centre**, at Jl Kartika Plaza 8X, Kuta Centre Block C 11 27–28, and Jl Raya Hang Tuah 11, Sanur (tel: 289481).

Timor Artshop, at Jl Legian 396B (tel: 751537), has a good range of Indonesian crafts. **Konsep Lama Kini**, at Jl Legian 427 (tel: 761197), has traditional items with a modern twist.

Left: rattan furniture maker
Right: a demon mask

Balinese Arts & Crafts

There are entire Balinese villages which produce both traditional and modern arts and crafts. The best place to find a good range is at the huge **Pasar Seni** (Art Market) in Sukawati with hundreds of small stalls. For those with time, here's a rundown of Balinese handicrafts and their sources:

Paintings: Works range from traditional to local interpretations of international trends. Many artists work from their homes. A good place for all styles is **Neka Gallery** (tel: 975034) in Ubud, across the main road from the post office.

Connoisseurs of modern art by both well-known Indonesian and international painters should not miss **Bamboo Gallery** (tel: 975037) along Jl Raya Ubud and **Komaneka Fine Art Gallery** (tel: 976090) in Monkey Forest Road.

Families in Kamasan, Klungkung, produce classical puppet-style paintings on canvas and various decorative objects. Drop by **Nyoman Mandra's Studio** (tel: 0366-21905) to watch him train young Balinese artists. For brightly-coloured works and beautiful hand-painted wooden eggs, see **Nyoman Arcana** (tel: 0366-23510) in Banjar Sangging.

Puppets: Flat figures with moveable arms are made from perforated and painted cattle hide. Many families in Banjar Babakan, Sukawati, create fine mythological figures, especially **Wayan Nartha** (tel: 299080).

Woodcarving: Be forewarned that most woods used for carving tend to crack in drier climates. Mas, Peliatan, Kemenuh and Buruan are major carving villages in Gianyar, producing figures of fishermen, farmers and bare-breasted women polished to a sheen. **Seraya Bali Style** (tel: 298572) in Batubulan sells a wide range of woodcrafts.

Modern pieces like colourful fruits, flowers and toys are sold at roadside stands in Tegalalang and Tengkulak. **Made Geriya Toy Makers** (tel: 975241) in Peliatan has a wide selection.

Carvings made from parasitic plants are environmentally-friendly as no trees are felled (removing the parasite saves a tree's life). Other materials used are coconut shells and cattle bones in Tampaksiring. Carved chess sets are a good buy here.

Also try: **Barong** in Mas (tel: 975807); **Citra Artshop** in Peliatan (tel: 975187); **Dastra Wood Carving** in Sukawati (tel: 298224); **Garuda Bali** in Batubulan (tel: 298535); **Kayangan Suci** in Mas (tel: 975245), **Sadu** in Peliatan (tel: 975023); and **Siadja** in Mas (tel: 975210).

Stone-carving: Mythological and modern figures are made from *paras* (compressed clay and ash), but due to their weight, packing and shipping them is expensive. Workshops line the roads along Batubulan in Gianyar and Penarukan in Tabanan. **Wayan Cemul** in Ubud is worth a visit for its creative pieces.

Jewellery: Look for gold jewellery in shops along Jl Hasanudin in Denpasar, and in major town markets. Bali is famous for silver jewellery made in Celuk, where shops like **Adiprana** (tel: 298129) and **Ketut Suardhana** (tel: 298241) line the roads.

Small places throughout Ubud have good selections; **Rai's Clothes 'n' Things** across the marketplace (tel: 977624) has unique designs and good textiles.

In Kuta-Legian, head for **Maharani Collection**, at Jl Raya Kuta 102 (tel: 751615); **Mario**, at Jl Melasti, Legian (tel: 753413); **Mirah Silver**, at Jl Tunjung Mekar 81, Kuta (tel: 754628); **Suarti**, at the Mastapa Garden Hotel, Jl Legian (tel: 751660); and **Yusuf Silver**, at Jl Legian Kelod 85 (tel: 752050).

A few boutiques offer pieces by Western designers, including **Just Jen's**, along Jl

Top: characters from the Hindu *Ramayana* epic
Right: tools of the puppet-making trade

Raya Seminyak, Kuta (tel: 731690). In Ubud, check out **Bagus**, along Jl Dewi Sita (tel: 976611), and **Seraphim**, in Jl Monkey Forest (tel: 973287).

Metalwork: Intricate tooled designs on pewter, brass and silver bowls for offerings are made by **Made Gita** next to *bale* Banjar Sangging in Kamasan, Klungkung. Used artillery cases are also worked with lovely motifs for use as vases.

Ceramics: Low-fired and fragile terracotta ritual wares available in most markets are made in Bedulu, Gianyar. Humorous figures and celadon-glazed porcelains are fashioned in Pejaten in Tabanan, and good-quality stoneware at Kapal, Badung.

Modern tableware (including designs made to order) is available in Kuta at **Rumah Manis**, Jl Nakula 9 (tel: 730606); **Jenggala**, Jl Uluwatu II, Jimbaran (tel: 703310/1); and **Sari Bumi**, Jl Danau Tamblingan 152, Sanur (tel: 287374).

Plant Fibre: Covered bamboo baskets are available in every marketplace. Rattan and palm-leaf baskets are made by **Mangku Made Gina** in Pengosekan.

Coiled baskets made of *ata* (liana) vines are a home industry in Tenganan, Karangasem. *Lontar* (palm-leaf books) are also made here, but better ones come from Sidemen.

Dried palm-leaf figures are fashioned in Bona, Gianyar, which is also the centre for bamboo furniture and wind chimes. Bamboo will crack in places with air-conditioning or cold and dry winters.

Leather: Most pieces are made in Java and are available in many shops, especially at Goa Gajah in Bedulu. In Kuta-Legian, check out: **Chok's**, Jl Tunjung Mekar 10, Kuta (tel: 752628); **Gecko**, Jl Raya Legian 406 (tel: 751386); **Intai Rainbow**, Jl Raya Kuta 49 (tel: 754615); **Mon Ami**, Jl Bumi Sari 7, Kuta (tel: 755732); and **Sila Koleksi**, Jl Legian Kelod 373 (tel: 751686).

Textiles: A wide selection of shimmering Balinese *endek* (weft resist single-*ikat* cloth) is available at the **Nogo Bali Ikat Centre**, at Jl Danau Tamblingan 98, Sanur (tel: 288765), and **Wardani**, along Jl Monkey Forest, Ubud (tel: 975538).

Better-quality *endek* cloths and *songket* (gold or silver brocade) are home industries at **Pelangi** (tel: 23012) in Sidemen, Karangasem, and in Gelgel, Klungkung. In Batuan, Blayu (Tabanan) and Negara (Jembrana), weavers make brocades with coloured threads. Beautiful silks are woven at **Pertenunan Berdikari**, at Jl Dewi Sartika 42, Singaraja (tel: 22217).

Geringsing (warp and weft resist, double *ikat*-patterned cloth) is produced only

in Tenganan, Karangasem. Prices run into the hundreds of US dollars for a new piece, and up to thousands for a museum-quality antique. Good pieces are available from **Wayan Kondri** and **Nyoman Diani**. Fine textiles from eastern Indonesia are also sold here, in Klungkung, and along Jl Gajah Mada, Denpasar.

Silk-screened gold cloths for fans and hangings are produced in Sukawati. Temple parasols are made in Satria, Klungkung. Tampaksiring (Gianyar) has fine crochet tablecloths and bedspreads.

Javanese batik is available at: **Keris**, at Galleria Nusa Dua (tel: 771303); **Danar Hadi**, Jl Legian Raya 113 (tel: 752164); **Mirota**, Jl Raya Tuban 3, Kuta (tel: 753758); **Surya Kencana** (tel: 298361), Banjar Sasih, Batubulan; and **Winotosastro**, Jl Sanur 102, Denpasar (tel: 223651).

Clothes

Department stores like **Matahari**, at Jl Dewi Sartika 4G, Denpasar (tel: 237364), **Plaza Bali**, at Jl Bypass Ngurah Rai, Tuban, Nusa Dua (tel: 753301), and **Galeria Nusa Dua** (tel: 771662) in Nusa Dua offer one-stop shopping for all kinds of clothing.

In Kuta alone hundreds of shops sell clothes. Check out: **Kuta Bali**, Jl Tunjung Mekar Gang Menuh (tel: 753693); **Milo's**, Kuta Square Block E1–1A (tel: 754081); **Mimi's**, Jl Oberoi (tel: 751732); **Nandie Amidarmo**, Jl Kartika Plaza (tel: 751555);

and **Wira's**, Jl Raya Kuta (tel: 751727).

For beach and sportswear, go to **Body Glove**, Kuta Centre A II 13–14 (tel: 753657).

Get children's clothing in Kuta at **Indigo Kids**, Jl Pantai Kuta (tel: 755265); **Kids A GoGo**, Jl Legian (tel: 752805); and **Kuta Kidz**, Jl Pantai Kuta (tel: 755810).

In Sanur, head for **Mama & Leon**, at Jl Hyatt 99A (tel: 288044). For beautiful handmade lacy fashions, check out **Uluwatu**, at Jl Danau Tamblingan (tel: 288977), with branches at Galeria Nusa Dua (tel: 771509), Jl Pantai Kuta (tel: 755542) and Jl Monkey Forest, Ubud (tel: 977557).

Look for ethnic fashions at **Daya**, along Jl Raya Seminyak, Kuta (tel: 733560) and Jl Monkey Forest, Ubud (tel: 977981).

Hotel Boutiques

If you prefer to shop in comfort and away from the heat and dust, make a beeline for up-market hotel boutiques. Things are always more expensive but you do find items sometimes not found elsewhere. **Four Seasons** resorts at Jimbaran and Sayan have a good range of ready-made clothes and expensive antiques; **Amandari** in Ubud for jewellery and high-quality antiques; **Amankila** in Candi Dasa for hand-crafted household goods; **Taman Burung** in Singapadu for exquisite wooden items; **Chedi** in Ubud for products made of natural materials; and **Oberoi** in Krobokan for exquisite jewellery and gifts.

Top: a Balinese weaver at work

EATING OUT

Real Balinese food is the traditional fare eaten at home and at *warung* (small roadside stalls). It is mainly rice, eaten with small portions of spicy vegetables, fish and meat, and accompanied by *sambal* (hot paste ground from fiery chillies). Balinese cooking favours the use of coconuts (either grated or as coconut milk), fresh spices, garlic, onions and chillies, so while the dishes are deliciously fragrant, they can also be tantalisingly hot.

Speciality Balinese dishes served at home on festive occasions, but which can also be ordered in advance at some restaurants, are *babi guling* (roast suckling pig), *bebek tutu* (duck wrapped in banana leaves and smoked overnight) and *lawar* (spicy minced vegetables or meat mixed with grated coconut and sometimes raw blood).

If you want to try genuine Balinese cooking, you have to either get invited to a Balinese home, or eat at a *warung*. At the latter, the food is usually delicious, but the standards of hygiene may be questionable.

In tourist restaurants, Indonesian dishes are usually watered-down affairs cooked to suit Western tastes – with less rice, more meat and milder spicing. These days, in addition to the repertoire of Indonesian and Chinese staples that are on most standard tourist menus, many restaurants are going international – serving up eclectic offerings such as sashimi, spaghetti Bolognese, Thai beef salad and chocolate mousse – to cater to visitors the world over.

As for thirst-quenchers, a good local beer to go with your food is Bintang, especially light and fresh. Other local brews to try are *tuak* (palm-beer, strange-tasting and intoxicating), *brem* (sweet rice wine) and *arak* (palm gin). The Balinese also make *anggur* (wine) from grapes. Imported liquors are available but are expensive due to high import taxes.

New restaurants open and close all the time. Most of the places listed in the pages that follow have been good for years, but there are, of course, many more worth discovering. Many hotels also have restaurants which serve good food but these are not listed here (see *Practical Information, pages 91–6*).

In the tourist centres of Sanur, Kuta-Legian and Nusa Dua, restaurants usually serve lunch from 11am–3pm, and dinner (some with dance performances) from 6–10pm daily. Except for 24-hour coffee shops in resort hotels, very few restaurants serve breakfast or keep very late hours.

In Ubud, Lovina and Candi Dusa, restaurants open from 11am–9pm daily. Small eating outlets for locals and more adventurous travellers are scattered everywhere, with varied opening times and menus, but these may not be very hygienic. Portable food carts operate along the roads but these may pose even greater health risks.

The following price categories are for a meal for two without drinks, but rates are lower at local eateries (under US$5 for two):
$ = under US$20
$$ = US$20–40
$$$ = over US$40

Telephone codes are given for each area. Jl (Jalan) means 'Street'.

Sanur (0361)
Canang Sari Restaurant
Jl Danau Batur 2, Sanur
Tel: 287027
Extensive selection of seafood along with Indonesian, European, Japanese, Chinese, Korean and vegetarian dishes. Exclusive dining with varied dance programme every night at 8pm. $$

Cafe Batujimbar
Jl Danau Tamblingan 152, Sanur
Tel: 287374

Right: Kuta street vendor

A long-time favourite of people who know Sanur. Fantastic salads and sandwiches; good vegetarian selection and organic food as well. $$

Legong Restaurant
Jl Danau Tamblingan 196, Sanur
Tel: 288066
Delicious Indonesian, Chinese and European cuisine with nightly dinner dance show at 8pm and friendly atmosphere. $$

Ronny's Restaurant
Jl Danau Tamblingan 202, Sanur
Tel: 288370
Still popular after many years, with excellent seafood, Chinese, Indonesian and international dishes. $$

Mezzanine Restaurant & Bar
Jl Danau Tamblingan 63, Sanur
Tel: 270624
One of the newest restaurants in the area; opened in August 2000. Features excellent fusion cuisine that marries together the best of the East and West. Two levels of seating and nightly entertainment. $$$

Trattoria da Marco
off Jl Mertasari, Sanur
Tel: 288966
For over 15 years, owners Reno and Diddit da Marco have maintained the restaurant's reputation for cooking excellent grilled fish, salads and pastas. $$

Warung Jawa Barat
Jl Danau Poso 10, Sanur
Tel: 288309
For West Javanese food and great grilled fish in a simple setting; a good place to mix with the locals. $

Kuta / Legian (0361)

For inexpensive and delicious grilled seafood at night, head for the **Kuta Night Market** and **Jimbaran Beach**. The food is inexpensive just as long as you avoid eating lobsters.

Aromas Restaurant
Camplung Mas, Legian
Tel: 751003
A peaceful garden setting away from the main road; excellent salads, exotic vegetarian dishes and great desserts. $$

Kori Restaurant & Bar
Jl Gang Poppies II, Kuta
Tel: 758605
Escape from the Kuta crowds to this quiet retreat with wonderful Balinese ambience. Serves international cuisine and freshly-grilled seafood as well as Balinese dishes. $$

Kuta Seafood Theatre & Restaurant
Jl Kartika Plaza 92X
Tel: 755807
Excellent Chinese seafood dishes in a huge dining hall (which can get noisy) with dance performances nightly at 8pm. $$

Made's Warung
Jl Pantai Kuta
Tel: 755297
One of the first places to cater to foreigners when it was one of only two eateries on Kuta's main street. Still popular with its menu of local and international dishes and delicious desserts, and a *rijstaffel* on Saturday nights. A new branch, Made's Warung II (tel: 732130) has opened in Seminyak. $$

Poppies Restaurant
Gang Poppies I, Kuta
Tel: 751059
An old favourite with a cozy garden setting and a good, varied menu. Get there early for a seat during peak tourist season. $$

TJ's Mexican Restaurant
Gang Poppies I
Tel: 751093
Serves the best *enchiladas*, *tacos*, *tostadas*, *nachos* and *margaritas* this side of the Pacific. Try the eggplant or *tahu*/bean dip with chips; great with a cold beer. $$

Warung Kopi
Jl Legian 427
Tel: 753602
Friendly atmosphere with central location and garden courtyard. Indian, Mediterranean and vegetarian cuisine; fabulous homemade desserts and ice-creams. $$

Seminyak (0361)
Gateway of India
Jl Abimanyu, Seminyak
Tel: 732-940
With an Indian owner married to a Balinese, you can be assured of authentic Indian fare. The tandoori dishes and the freshly-baked *naan* breads are simply wonderful. $

Kafe Warisan
Jl Kerobokan Banjar Taman 68
Tel: 731175
A favourite on the island and featured widely in the international press. French and Algerian restaurateurs dish up fresh, light and tasty fare with a French leaning. Open from 6.30pm. Reservations essential, especially if you want to dine under the stars in the courtyard terrace. $$$

Ku dé Ta
Jl Laksmana, Petitenget
Tel: 736969
This upmarket restaurant has received rave reviews since its opening in December 2000. Beautiful beachside location and spiffy waiters dressed in black bring sophistication to the Seminyak dining scene. Australian chef Chris Patzold serves modern Australian dishes given an Asian twist. $$$

La Lucciola Restaurant & Bar
Jl Laksmana, Petitenget
Tel: 261047
Delicious Mediterranean food and a casual atmosphere are the hallmarks of this big, two-level thatched structure which looks out over the beach. Also offers beachfront chairs and massage during the day. Great for sunset cocktails and packed for dinner. Reservations essential, otherwise expect to wait at least an hour for a table. $$

Warung Batavia
Jl Seminyak
Tel: 73164
Serves delightful *betawi* – Jakarta-style – fare, including *nasi campur* (mixed rice with lots of side dishes), *soto* chicken soup and *gado-gado* (steamed vegetable salad with spicy peanut sauce). $

Nusa Dua / Tanjung Benoa (0361)
Mentari Ming Garden Bar & Restaurant
Jl Pantai Mengiat, Nusa Dua
Tel: 772125
Tasty Chinese cuisine, seafood and a varied Indonesian buffet served in a lovely garden setting. $$

Pantai Mina Brasserie
Jl Pratama 216, Tanjung Benoa
Tel: 773812
By the beach serving grilled seafood, Asian and European cuisines. $$$

Rayunan International Bar & Restaurant
Galleria Nusa Dua, Block E, No 2
Tel: 775698
Chinese, Indian and European dishes served in a garden or indoors, and delicious cakes and pastries. Live entertainment nightly at 7pm with parade of Balinese dancers. $$

Left: Poppies Restaurant at Kuta

Ulam
Jl Pantai Mengiat 14, Nusa Dua
Tel: 771590, 773776
People come from far away for some of the tastiest grilled seafood with Balinese spices. $$

Denpasar (0361)
Atoom Baru
Jl Gajah Mada 106–108
Tel: 222623
Favourite with locals for Chinese food; lots of street noise, but good place to stop if exploring the nearby marketplace. $

Rumah Makan Betty
Jl Sumatra 56
Tel: 224502
Good range of Indonesian and Chinese food. Try their *tahu goreng telur* (fried tofu and eggs), *nasi campur* (rice with several side dishes) and *bubur ayam* (rice porridge with chicken). $

Satria Rumah Makan
Jl Kedondong 11
Tel: 235993
Good Balinese food near Pasar Satria bird market; very popular with locals. $

Ubud (0361)
Ary's Warung
Jl Raya Ubud
Tel: 975053
Has some of the best fare on the island. The food is of a high standard, and is reasonably priced. Taking in the neighbouring *banjar*, a new two-level bar and dining terrace offers a breezy atmosphere.

Bebek Bengil (Dirty Duck)
Jl Hanuman, Padangtegal
Tel: 975489
Enjoy some of Bali's best nouvelle cuisine and desserts next to the rice fields. Breezy atmosphere with scenic views of Gunung Agung. $$

Café Wayan
Monkey Forest Road
Tel: 975063
Excellent fusion food and delicious desserts in a garden setting with semi-private pavilions. Ibu Wayan was trained in California and is especially good with cakes and pastries. $$

Casa Luna
Jl Raya Ubud
Tel: 976283
Feast on great food and desserts in a cozy setting, with nightly screenings of films; also conducts cooking classes from 10am–2pm Monday–Wednesday but there has to be a minimum of five persons. $$

Griya Barbecue
Jl Raya Ubud
Tel: 975428
Famous for the tastiest barbecued seafood and meat in town. Ask for a table in the room at the back which has stunning views of the gorge. $$

Kampung Café
Ceking, Tegalalang, Gianyar
Tel: 901201
Enjoy exquisite views of rice terraces while feasting on delicious European and Asian nouvelle cuisine. $$

Kokokan Bar & Restaurant
Hotel Kokokan
Pengosekan, Ubud
Tel: 975742
Deliciously spicy Thai food and a bar set in a large open-sided pavilion. The service however can be a trifle slow. $$$

Left: cafes are a popular hangout

Lotus Café
Jl RayaUbud
Tel: 975660
Housed in a charming open-air courtyard; ask for a table next to the lotus pond with a replica temple. Delicious pastas and yummy cheesecakes and brownies. $$

Murni's
Campuhan Bridge
Tel: 975233
One of the first places to cater to foreigners with Indonesian and Western food, and desserts in a setting above the river. There are three levels of seating and overlooks the Campuhan river. $$

Lovina / Buleleng (0362)
Damai Lovina Villas
Jl Damai, Kayuputih, Lovina
Tel: 41008
Restaurant is located in a small villa-style hotel on the mountain slopes outside of Lovina town. Exquisite cuisine using fresh Balinese ingredients. Prepared by an award-winning Danish chef. $$$

Kakatua
Kalibukbuk, Lovina
Tel: 41344
Excellent seafood served in a large open pavilion. Also serves an eclectic mix of Mexican, Thai and Indian dishes. $

Khi Khi Seafood Restaurant
Kalibukbuk, Lovina
Tel: 41548
Famous for its grilled fish, fresh from the waters nearby, and the marvellous sauces which go with it. $

Rumah Makan Arina
Jl A Yani 53, Singaraja
Tel: 23209
Located right in the centre of town, with tasty Chinese and Indonesian food. The *mie goreng* (fried noodles) are especially good. $

Candi Dasa / Karangasem (0363)
Ibu Rasmini's Warung
Jl Raya Candi Dasa
Tasty meals in a small place just past the lagoon on the other side of the road. Offers good value for money. $

Kubu Bali
Jl Raya Candi Dasa
Popular restaurant specialising in fresh seafood; has an open kitchen. $

Sacred Mountain Restaurant
Banjar Budamanis, Sidemen, Karangasem
Tel: 24330
Situated on the bank of a river, this is one of the most serene spots for a meal. Ask for a table with a view. $$

Above: an Indonesian-style curry and rice meal

NIGHTLIFE

There is no throbbing nightlife scene to speak of in Bali. Denpasar has a small complex of four movie theatres at **Wisata Cini-plex** on Jalan Thamrin, showing mostly Hollywood films three to six months after their release in the United States.

The main discos in Kuta-Legian change in popularity from one year to the next, catering mostly to young holiday-seeking Indonesians from Jakarta, Westerners (especially Australians) and Japanese. Most of these places don't get going till after 1am.

Infamous 'pub-crawls' take bar-goers from one drinking place to another all night long until dawn. Some of them get so stoned drunk that they wind up sleeping along the beach and roadsides, but this exposes them to the elements and thieves.

The Sanur scene is more relaxed with a few low-key discos that attract a sophisticated and mature crowd. Discos in luxury class Nusa Dua hotels are popular with some locals and tourists, but they are very exclusive and expensive.

Ubud, by village regulations to protect the morals of its youth, does not have any discos and only offers nightly Balinese cultural dance programmes that usually finish by 9pm (see *Practical Information, page 97*). A few restaurant-bars in the area close by 11pm, so most tourists in Ubud go to bed early and rise with the sun to explore the countryside instead.

Many late-night temple ceremonies with performances happen in the Ubud area or at villages within reasonable distances by car or motorcycle (see *Calendar of Events, pages 83–5*).

Below are some of the more popular places. Some are full-service restaurants that also feature pubs and live music. Note: Jl (Jalan) means 'Street'.

Kuta-Legian
Bali Rock Café
Jl Melasti 666, Kuta
Tel: 754466
Fun place with party themes, good food and live music.

BB Discotheque
Ramada Bintang Bali Resort
Jl Kartika Plaza, Tuban
Tel: 753292
Roomy dance floor and flashing lights attract a more sophisticated crowd; includes karaoke lounge and bar.

Café del Mar
Jl Abimanyu 100X, Seminyak
Tel: 734298
Plays a variety of music, and has the coolest tropical open-air bar in Bali.

Café Luna
Jl Raya Seminyak, Kuta
Tel: 730805
Good food, bar and dancing to live music on Tuesday and Thursday nights, 9.30pm–midnight.

Casablanca
Jalan Bunisari, Kuta
Tel: 751333
Lively Australian-style bar filled to the brim on most nights.

The Club At The Villas
Jl Kunti 118x, Seminyak
Tel: 730840
Latest trendy indoor nightclub, fully air-conditioned with dance music from 1am till after the sun rises. A very happening place at the moment.

Double Six
Jl Arjuna, Seminyak
Tel: 753666
Sophisticated mature crowds come here late for lots of action with frenetic dancing to techno and trance music in an open-air place. Cover charge includes one free drink. You can even bungy-jump during club hours.

Gado-Gado
Jl Dhyana Pura, Kuta
Tel: 752255
This open-air place is very popular with more mature crowds of locals and expatriates. After midnight, things really start to swing. Cover charge includes a free drink.

Glory
Jl Legian Kaja 445
Tel: 751091
Features European, Indonesian and Chinese cuisine; bar open till midnight.

Goa 2001
Jl Legian
Tel: 753922
Also a restaurant serving decent Indian curries and tandoori dishes, it is better known for its bar. An established favourite watering-hole for young locals.

Hard Rock Café
Jl Pantai Kuta
Tel: 755661
A very funky place located right on the beach, with great party atmosphere and good live music. Bands change every few weeks. Also a restaurant serving great burgers, steak and fries before 10pm.

The Jaya Pub
Jl Seminyak 21, Kuta
Tel: 730973
Popular for its late-night band and casual atmosphere.

Peanuts
Jalan Legian
Tel: 754149
Popular with a young crowd; features wide-screen videos, flashing lights and pounding music. Both live bands and deejay music.

Santa Fe Bar & Grill
Jl Abimanyu 11A, Seminyak, Kuta
Tel: 731147
Relaxing and popular place for Indonesian, Mexican and European food. Live music on Monday, Tuesday, Thursday and Saturday.

Sari Club
Jl Legian, Kuta
Tel: 754903
Offers reasonably-priced drinks, but very crowded and noisy after 9pm. One of the more established spots in town.

Nusa Dua
Club Tabuh
Nusa Dua Beach Hotel
Tel: 771201

Left: a Sanur band
Above: tropical cooler

This elegant and expensive disco is mostly frequented by hotel guests and a more sophisticated local crowd. Features jazz, Caribbean and Latino sounds from 9pm–1am.

Oasis
Jl Bypass Ngurah Rai, Jimbaran
Tel: 702669, 702686
Open for lunch and dinner with live jazz and blues from Thursday to Saturday nights starting at 10pm.

Octopus
Hilton Hotel, Nusa Dua
Tel: 771102
Spacious upscale disco for sophisticated crowds and hotel guests seeking a more relaxed atmosphere.

Poco Loco
Jl Pantai Mengiat, Nusa Dua
Tel: 773923
Jl Padma Utara, Legian
Tel: 756079
Two different locations to enjoy prize-winning Mexican food and frozen magaritas, with complete bar. Lively and friendly atmosphere and open till 4am.

Sanur
Janger
Jl Danau Tamblingan 21
Tel: 288888
Popular disco that stays open all night long, sometimes until the sun rises. Plenty of experienced bar staff can make any drink you want.

Kafe Wayang Bar & Restaurant
Komplek Sanur Raya 12–14
Tel: 287591
Enjoy delicious Asian-Mediterranean fusion cuisine in cozy surroundings, with funky live music on Friday and Saturday nights starting at 9pm.

Peppers Bar
Hotel Sanur Beach
Jl Danau Tamblingan
Tel: 288011
Latino bar and restaurant with hot live music; free salsa dance lessons on Saturday at 11am. Great atmosphere, stays open till 2am.

Planet Sanur Café
Jl Danau Tamblingan 202
Tel: 287597
Enjoy great food, cocktails, live music, and lots of fun till late night hours.

Ubud
Batan Waru
Jl Dewi Sita
Tel: 977528
Popular watering-hole for locals and expatriates with world music, hip-hop and acid jazz till midnight.

Café Exiles
Jl Pengosekan
Tel: 974812
Attracts a mixed crowd looking for an offbeat late night scene.

Funky Monkey Cafe & Music Bar
Jl Monkey Forest
Tel: 903729
Plays the whole spectrum from jazz to world music and garage. Special theme nights.

Jazz Café
Jl Tebasaya
No telephone
Outstanding local musicians play acoustic jazz on Wednesday, Friday and Saturday.

Sai Sai Bar
Jl Monkey Forest
Tel: 975570
Only place in town with live music; popular with locals and tourists but closes at 11pm.

Top: relaxing at Bali Hyatt's bar

CALENDAR OF EVENTS

Temple festivals are a good opportunity to see Bali in its ceremonial splendour. The Balinese follow two different calendars. The *Saka* solar-lunar year begins in AD 78 (1923 starts in March 2001) and has 354 days with a 13th month added once every three years. The *Pawukon* cycle of 210 days repeats unnumbered and has concurrently running periods of one to 10 days, the conjunctions of which determine the *odalan* (temple festivals). Together, these two parallel calendar systems determine the incredibly complex schedule of holy days and anniversaries celebrated throughout Bali.

Visitors to a *pura* (temple) should dress properly for a festival in long hip-cloth, sash and sleeved shirt, with men adding a folded head-cloth and short overskirt. Events usually start in the late afternoon and last throughout the night, especially performances. Don't climb on any structure to take photographs and avoid using a flash as it distracts the priests and worshippers.

At popular temples, expect to pay an entry fee (Rp1,050), adding more for a camera (Rp500) or video (Rp1,000). Otherwise, a donation of Rp2,000 per person is common. Menstruating women and anyone with an open wound are not allowed to enter because of a taboo associated with blood.

Lunar Festivals

Events that begin at *purnama* (full moon) are indicated by a red spot above the date on a printed Balinese calendar, while *tilem* (new moon) festivals by a black spot. A detailed calendar can be obtained from the local tourism offices (see *Practical Information, page 98*). Lunar months approximately are as follows:

December / January
Tilem: Vigils held in temples on *Siwalatri* (Night of Shiva), the night before *tilem*.

January / February
Purnama: Prayers in the mist-filled **Pura Dalem** (Batur, Kintamani).

February / March
Purnama: **Pura Penataran Sasih** (Pejeng) has processions of visiting deities, beautiful offerings and ritual dances and battles.
Tilem: A few days before the new moon, temple images are carried in procession to the sea coast for *melasti* (ritual cleansing). Watch at Jalan Segara Ayu and Padang Galak (Sanur), Kuta-Legian, Purnama (Sukawati), Lebih (Gianyar) and Batu Klotok (Klungkung).

On *tilem*, exorcism sacrifices take place at the major crossroads in every village and

Above: festival offerings

town. The evening is noisy with demons being chased out from households, and *ogoh-ogoh* (monstrous effigies) carried around the streets with torches.

The next morning is New Year's Day or Nyepi, a day of complete silence. No fires are lit, no work is done, and it's forbidden to go outside, so stay indoors at your hotel.

March / April
Purnama: Huge 11-day festivals begin at **Pura Penataran Agung** (Besakih) and **Pura Ulun Danu** (Batur), with ritual dances and worshippers from everywhere.

April / May
Purnama: **Pura Samuan Tiga** (Bedulu) has processions along with ceremonial dances and ritual battles during a 13-day ceremony.

May / June
Purnama: 11 days of rituals begin at **Pura Agung Batan Bingin** (Pejeng).

June / July
Purnama: **Pura Penataran Agung** (Sukawati) has a procession with girls and women in elaborate outfits.

Makare battles in which thorny pandanus leaves are used to draw blood take place in Tenganan (Karangasem). Dates are set by yet another calendar. The cremation season

begins and continues through September.

Pesta Kesenian Bali (Bali Arts Festival) held at the Art Centre in Denpasar. The opening day features a huge procession. Obtain schedules from tourist offices.

July / August
Purnama: Beautiful offerings brought to **Pura Pusering Jagat** and **Pura Pengukur-ukuran** (Pejeng).

August / September
Purnama: **Pura Gunung Kawi** (Tampaksiring) features beautiful offerings and colourful ritual dances.

September / October
Purnama: **Pura Tirta Empul** (Tampaksiring) has tall offerings. **Goa Gajah** (Bedulu) begins an 11-day celebration. **Pura Dasar** (Gelgel, Klungkung) receives visiting deities. Beautiful offerings at **Pura Desa** (Ulakan, Karangasem).

October / November
Purnama: Trance celebrations with bloodletting and ritual dances at **Pura Desa** (Sengkidu, Karangasem).

November / December
Tilem: Seaside ceremonies at **Lebih** (Gianyar) and **Purnama** (Sukawati).

Above: a cremation ceremony in progress

Pawukon Festivals

Dates vary for events and *tumpek* (ceremonies honouring special objects):

Tumpek Landep

Celebration for metal objects, especially *keris* (daggers), but even motorised vehicles are given offerings and decorated with palm-leaf ornaments; metal smiths pray at **Pura Ratu Pande** (Besakih): 28 July 2001; 23 February/21 September 2002.

Tumpek Wariga or Uduh

Offerings tied around fruiting trees; ceremonial dances at **Pura Desa** (Batuan): 3 February/1 September 2001; 30 March/26 October 2002.

Note: Add the prescribed number of days to the given dates to calculate festivals at the following temples:

+10: **Danu Bratan** (Bedugul) on the lake's edge.
+11: **Pura Pucaksari** (Sangeh) with scores of monkeys.

Tumpek Krulut

Celebration for singing birds and musical instruments: 14 April/10 November 2001; 8 June 2002.

+4: **Pura Peti Tenget** (Kerobokan, Kuta) has a spooky atmosphere.
+10: One of three **Pura Dalem** (Sukawati-Batuan) has processions of women in festive dress.

Tumpek Uye or Kandang

Rituals for domestic animals, especially sacred albino cattle in Taro (Payangan); music and dance at **Pura Kebo Edan** (Pejeng): 19 May/15 December 2001; 13 July 2002; 8 February/6 September 2003.

Tumpek Wayang

Ceremonies for sacred puppets, including masks like the one at **Pura Samuan Tiga** (Bedulu): 23 June 2001; 19 January /17 August 2002.

+4: **Pura Basukian** (Besakih) for Basuki, serpent of wealth; **Pura Dalem Peed** (pronouced 'puh-aid'; Nusa Penida) for practitioners of black magic.

Hari Raya Saraswati

At end of the Pawukon cycle, Saraswati, goddess of knowledge, is honoured. Books are given offerings, reading and writing are not allowed, students pray at schools, and clients bring offerings to healers and priests: 14 July 2001; 9 February/7 September 2002.

+4: **Pura Payogan Agung** (Ketewel, Sukawati) holds unusual sacred masked dances. **Pura Kehen** (Bangli) has processions of offerings and ritual dances.

Galungan

Considered the most important of the Balinese festivals. Deified ancestors descend from heaven and visit for five days during this island-wide celebration. Pigs are slaughtered for offerings, temples are festooned with decorations, tall *penjor* (decorative bamboo poles) erected along roadsides and ritual feasting takes place at home: Festival dates are as follows: 28 February/26 September 2001; 24 April/20 November 2002.

+1: At **Pura Batukau** (Tabanan), worshippers may get possessed by tiger spirits.
+10: **Tumpek Kuningan** ceremony for household tools, and new offerings made everywhere. At **Pura Hyang Api** (Kelusa, Payangan), hundreds of small cockfights take place outside the temple. Colourful festival at **Pura Taman Pule** (Mas); trance at **Pura Sakenan** (Pulau Serangan); exciting battle of the deities with trance at **Pura Timbrah** (Paksabali, Klungkung).
+14: Worshippers cross shallow waters for a festival at **Pura Tanah Lot** (Tabanan).

Pengerebongan

At **Pura Petilan** (Kesiman, Denpasar), dozens of holy images and sacred masks arrive in the early afternoon, then scores of people fall into trance: 18 March/14 October 2001; 12 May/8 December 2002.

+2: Processions of offerings to **Pura Taman Ayun** (Mengwi); spectacular setting at **Pura Ulu Watu** (Bukit Badung); prayers amidst bats at **Pura Goa Lawah** (Kusamba).

Practical Information

GETTING THERE

By Air

The only practical way to get to Bali is by air, although it is possible to arrive by ferry from Java and Lombok (see below), but not by sea from foreign destinations. Ngurah Rai International Airport, south of Denpasar, is also served by daily flights from Jakarta, Yogyakarta and other domestic locations.

International flights arrive directly from major Australian and Japanese cities, Seoul, Taipei, Hong Kong and Kuala Lumpur, while flights from Singapore and Bangkok also bring transit passengers from Europe and the United States. Many other airlines fly only to Jakarta, where transfer is made to a 90-minute domestic flight to Bali.

Ferry

Inter-island ferries ply the 30-minute trip between Gilimanuk in Jembrana (West Bali) and Ketapang in East Java. From Pandang-bai in Karangasem (East Bali), ferries take 4 hours to reach Lembar in Lombok.

TRAVEL ESSENTIALS

When to Visit

Peak tourist periods are June–August and December–January, so the best times to visit are April–May and September, when hotels are not full and may offer lower rates.

Visas & Passports

Passport must be valid for at least six months from the date of departure and you must have a confirmed ticket out. Two-month tourist visas are issued upon arrival for nationals from most ASEAN countries (Brunei, Malaysia, Philippines, Singapore, Thailand, Vietnam), Australia, New Zealand, Canada, the US and Western European countries. Visitors from other countries must apply at an Indonesian consulate or embassy abroad.

Left: friendly encounters in Bali
Right: Denpasar airport

Vaccinations

International health certificates of vaccination against smallpox, cholera and yellow fever are required only for travellers coming from infected areas. Typhoid vaccinations and Hepatitis A and B inoculations are recommended.

Customs

You are allowed to bring in 2 litres of alcoholic beverages, 200 cigarettes (50 cigars or 100g of tobacco), and a reasonable amount of perfume. Pre-recorded videos, pornography and weapons are not allowed. There are stiff penalties and long prison sentences for narcotics. On departure, up to Rp5 million may be taken out. Items more than 50 years old may not be exported.

Weather

The cool and dry (23–29°C) season is from May–September, but colder in the mountains at night. The hot and rainy (24–31°C) season lasts from November–March, with short thunderstorms in the late afternoon. April and October are transitional months.

Clothing

Bring casual clothes of lightweight natural fabrics for comfort in the heat and the humidity, or buy them in Bali. In more conservative areas such as Sanur, Ubud and other places inland, women will be more comfortable dressed in a medium length skirt and sleeved shirt.

Electricity

Indonesia uses a 220-volt system, and power failures are common, but major hotels have their own generators.

Time Differences

There are three time zones in Indonesia. Bali is in the Central Indonesian Time (WITA) zone, 1 hour ahead of Java and 8 hours ahead of Greenwich Mean Time.

GETTING ACQUAINTED

Geography

Bali is 8 degrees south of the equator and 115 degrees east longitude. As one of nearly 14,000 islands in Indonesia, it is located midway in the archipelago and covers 5,600sq km (2,021sq miles). Gunung Agung, which last erupted in 1963, is Bali's highest mountain at 3,142m (10,300ft). The immense crater of Gunung Batur at 1,717m (5,633ft) holds a lake that flows out to most of the rivers, as do three smaller lakes from mountains in the Bratan area.

Government & Economy

Bali is one of Indonesia's 26 provinces headed by an appointed governor. It is divided into the municipality of Denpasar, the provincial capital headed by a mayor, and eight *kabupaten* (regencies) roughly corresponding geographically to kingdoms of pre-colonial times: Badung, Bangli, Buleleng, Gianyar, Karangasem, Klungkung (Semarapura), Negara, and Tabanan. Each is headed by a locally-elected *bupati* (regent).

Tourism has played an important role in Bali's economy since the 1920s. Indonesia's First Five-Year Development Plan used the island's exotic image as the focus for tourism.

Infrastructure improvements led to spectacular economic growth, and Bali now has one of the nation's highest average income levels.

Although many Balinese are employed in the tourism sector, most still work as farmers, small traders and in local businesses. Industries related to or benefiting from tourism – garments, arts and crafts, construction – keep thousands of people employed in low-paying jobs. Even the agricultural sector is becoming tourist-oriented with the growing of flowers and produce for hotels and restaurants.

Rice takes up most arable land, with two to three crops per year, while coffee and cloves are grown on small plantations. However, increasing amounts of acreage are being converted to tract housing, luxury hotels, golf courses, roads and recreational developments. This puts enormous environmental stresses on the limited land and water resources on the densely-populated island.

Religion

Most Balinese follow a kind of Hinduism mixed with Buddhism, animism, magic and ancestor worship. Religious ceremonies take place nearly every day of the year.

There are small groups of Christians, Buddhists and Muslims. As a minority in predominantly Islamic Indonesia, the Balinese have a strong sense of ethnic, religious and cultural identity.

Language

The Indonesian language, Bahasa Indonesia, is the national language of the Republic of Indonesia but the indigenous languages of the archipelago are still very much alive, especially in Bali. Indonesian is used in the schools, by the government, and increasingly in commerce and in tourism. Many people speak a bit of English.

The complex Balinese language, Bahasa Bali, is very intrinsic to the culture, with several language levels in which are whole clusters of alternative vocabularies reflecting differences in rank. If you should pick up a few words of Balinese, be aware that you run the risk of offending someone if the rank distinction is not observed. Still, a useful phrasebook like the *Speak Indonesian* by Sylvia Tiwon will help you get off to a good start.

Above: well signposted for visitors

How Not To Offend

Use the right hand to give and receive things. If you must point, use your right thumb and never with your foot. A person's head is sacred, and don't even touch a child's head in affection. Steamy kissing and necking are offensive and forbidden in temples.

Visitors to a *pura* (temple) should dress properly for a festival in long hip-cloth, sash and sleeved shirt, with men adding a folded head-cloth and short overskirt. If visiting a temple on non-festival days, sleeved shirts and long trousers or skirts are sufficient, but a sash is required. Many temples will loan a sash for a fee, but it's easier to carry one with you. Don't climb on any structure, even a wall, to take photographs and avoid using a flash as it distracts the worshippers. Menstruating women and anyone with an open wound are fobidden to enter temples because of a taboo associated with blood. Wear swimwear only on the beach. Nude or topless sunbathing is impolite and even illegal.

People

Most of the island's nearly 3 million inhabitants are ethnic Balinese. A few villages, like Trunyan and Tenganan, are populated by the Bali Aga, who claim to be the original inhabitants before the Javanese came. There are small groups of migrant workers – mainly vendors from Java and Lombok while the Chinese are found in cities and larger towns, mostly running businesses.

MONEY MATTERS

Currency

The Indonesian monetary unit is the *rupiah*, (a little over Rp8,000 to US$1 at press time, with daily fluctuations in the exchange rate). Currency notes are in denominations of Rp100, Rp500, Rp1,000, Rp5,000, Rp10,000, Rp20,000, Rp50,000, and Rp100,000. Coins are in Rp25, Rp50, Rp100, Rp500, and Rp1,000. Carry smaller notes in case people can't give you change.

Foreign currency and travellers' cheques can be exchanged at the airport, banks and money-changers in the major tourist centres.

Credit Cards / Cash Machines

Most large hotels, restaurants and shops accept major credit cards, but may add another 3–5 percent to the bill. Most cash machines are for local banks, but cash advances using major credit cards can be obtained from most of the larger banks in Denpasar and major tourist centres.

Taxes / Tipping

Most hotels and restaurants in tourist centres levy a government tax and service charge ranging from 10–21 percent. Tipping is not common, but if someone gives extra good service, a tip is appreciated. Art shops give up to 30 percent commissions to guides and drivers who accompany you, which will add to the price of your purchase.

Above: a variety of headgear

Tip porters at hotels and the airport Rp1,000 per bag, more if it's big and heavy. International flight tax is Rp50,000; domestic flight tax is Rp11,000.

Banks / Money-changers

Banks are open 8.30am–2pm from Monday to Thursday, and 8.30–11am on Friday. Money-changers give better currency exchange rates and line the streets of major tourist centres, often staying open in the evening or until they run out of *rupiah*; be careful of those charging a commission fee. Large denomination US$ notes get a higher rate. Shop around for the best rate only if you need to change a lot of money to make it worthwhile.

GETTING AROUND

Taxis

Major hotels provide their own transfer services. Airport taxis are available from **Ngurah Rai Taxi** (tel: 724724), **Taxi Praja** (tel: 289090) and **Bali Taxi** (tel: 701111).

Public Transport

If you're not in a hurry and don't mind the loud music, and being crammed in with people, goods and sometimes livestock, just wait along the roadside and wave your hand to flag down a *bemo* (minivan), indicated by a yellow licence plate.

Routes are fixed and indicated by vehicle colour, so ask the driver or passengers. Although inexpensive, you will probably pay a little more as a tourist, but it's worth the experience to mix with the locals. Service is infrequent, mostly from 6am–6pm.

Car / Minivan

Hiring a car with driver is a very good idea, as it is not too expensive. Drivers know how to handle the hazardous main roads and narrow village lanes and can ask for directions, allowing you to relax and enjoy the scenery.

Vehicles are available through major hotels, tour agents or rental agencies, and insurance is available. Rates vary depending on the year and model. Shop around for a good deal, and ask if there is any special package. An international driver's licence is required if you want to do your own driving. Drive on the left side of the road. The following rental agencies are recommended:

Sanur: **Bagus Car Rental**, Jl Duyung 1, Sanur, tel: 287794; **Bali Jasa Utama**, Jl Danau Poso 46, Sanur, tel: 287370; **Hertz**, Grand Bali Beach, Sanur, tel: 288511.
Kuta: **Mega Jaya**, Jl Raya Kuta 78X, tel: 753760; **Star**, Jl Legian 4, Kuta, 730565; **Hertz**, Hotel Patra Jasa Bali, Kuta, tel: 751161.
Nusa Dua: **Hertz**, Hotel Putri Bali, Nusa Dua, tel: 771010; **Golden Bird Bali**, Jl Bypass Ngurah Rai, Nusa Dua, tel: 756170.
Ubud: **Dwi Tunggal**, Padangtegal, Ubud, tel: 976301.

Independent drivers congregate at waiting places in main tourist centres. Negotiate with the driver; tell him your itineraries and how long you expect to be out. (A 5-hour tour cost about Rp150,000 at time of press.) Clarify whether this includes petrol. A driver usually finds his own lunch, but you may ask him to join you.

Motorcycle

Numerous agencies, tour agents and hotels have motorcycles for hire. They will help arrange for a permit if your international driver's licence isn't endorsed for motorcycles. Rates vary according to year and model.

A helmet is required by law. Wear protective glasses around dusk to keep bugs out of your eyes, and a waterproof jacket in the cooler and wetter mountain areas. Use your horn to pass vehicles and to warn pedestrians. Beware of potholes and unmarked piles of sand and gravel along the roadsides, especially at night.

Left: local transport

HOURS & HOLIDAYS

Business Hours

Government offices are open 8am–2pm from Monday to Thursday, 8–11am on Friday, and 8am–1pm on Saturday. Get there early if you want to get anything done. Private business hours vary, but are generally from 9am–9pm. Some shops in Denpasar may close from 2–5pm.

Village marketplaces open very early in the morning and become deserted by noon, although some of the larger ones in the towns and cities remain fairly busy, with different vendors setting up temporary stalls in the late afternoon for night markets.

Public Holidays

Islamic holy days, Christian feast days (Good Friday) Buddha's birthday (full moon in May) and Hindu New Year's Day (day after the new moon in March) have variable dates and are public holidays. See *Calendar of Events, page 83–5* for other Balinese holy days.

Only these public holidays are fixed: **New Year's Day** (January 1), **Indonesian Independence Day** (August 17) and **Christmas Day** (December 25).

ACCOMMODATION

There is a wide range of accommodations in Bali – from over-the-top luxury hotels to very cheap homestays (also known as *losmen*). Most top-end hotels in Kuta, Jimbaran, Sanur and Nusa Dua are located on the beach and are of international standards. Many places have slightly higher rates during the peak tourist season from July to August, and from mid-December to mid-January. Reservations are recommended for the larger hotels during these peak periods. In the low season negotiate for lower rates. Deluxe and luxury accommodations will include hot water, air-conditioning, and usually IDD telephone and other facilities. Budget and economy places often include a simple breakfast.

The following symbols indicate price ranges (based on rack rates) for single occupancy and are subject to a 10–21 percent government tax and service charge:

$	=	under US$60
$$	=	US$60–120
$$$	=	US$120–200
$$$$	=	over US$200

Telephone codes are given for each area.

Kuta / Legian (0361)

Located in South Bali, near the airport. A crowded and noisy area but popular with visitors who want to be in the thick of things. Famous for surf and the beach, and gorgeous sunsets. Lots of shopping and boisterous nightlife. The Kuta stretch merges into Legian and Seminyak, where several exclusive resorts are located.

Barong Cottages
Jl Gang Poppies II, Kuta
Tel: 751804; Fax: 751520
Charming two-storey complex near the beach; it's central and has lovely gardens and two swimming pools. Good value for money. $

Hard Rock Beach Club
Jl Kuta Beach, Kuta
Tel: 761869, Fax: 761868
Definitely for the young or young-at-heart; 421 rooms and suites on the site of the very first hotel in Kuta. High energy fun, incorporating Hard Rock Café and seven other food and bar outlets, live entertainment daily. Not the place for quiet relaxation but great for families and fun. $$$

Legian Beach Hotel
Jl Melasti, Legian
Tel: 751711; Fax: 752652
Large complex with 217 rooms wrapped in a relaxed atmosphere near the beach, the hotel offers free airport transport and tour service. $$

Poppies Cottages I
Gang Poppies I, Kuta
Tel: 751059; Fax: 752364
Elegant bungalows set in private gardens with lily ponds and waterfalls, away from the beach. Other facilities include a swimming pool, CD library, games corner and garden restaurant. Often filled to capacity; reservations essential. $$

Ramada Bintang Bali Resort
Jl Kartika Plaza, Kuta
Tel: 753292, 753810; Fax: 753288
Comfortable beachside resort with a restful atmosphere and a full range of dining and recreational facilities. $$

Seminyak / Petitenget and Canggu (0361)
These are quieter beachfront areas north of the frenetic Kuta-Legian area, and featuring the same rough surf and brilliant sunsets. A variety of accommodation is available, from exclusive all-suite hotels to a number of intermediate range bungalows and cheap *losmen*.

Hotel Intan Bali
Jl Peti tenget, Kerobokan
Tel: 730777; Fax: 730778
Billed as a home away from home, with beautifully-landscaped gardens, beachside restaurants, pools, gym and spa. $$

Hotel Tugu Bali
Batu Bolong, Canggu
Tel: 731701; Fax: 731704
A boutique-style hotel with romantic villas embellished with art and antiques, and set in tropical gardens with lotus pools. Rather remote location on Canggu beach, where surfers congregate to catch the 'big one'. $$$$

The Legian
Jl Kayu Aya, Petitenget
Tel: 730622; Fax: 731291
Part of the upmarket GHM hotel group, this low-rise hotel on the beach has 71 luxurious sea-facing suites, featuring satellite television and CD sound system. Sophisticated modern Balinese architectural style with

pool and bar, excellent restaurant, library, meeting room, and free shuttle to Kuta. $$$$

The Oberoi
Jl Kayu Aya, Petitenget
Tel: 730361; Fax: 730791
This exclusive hotel along one of Bali's finest beaches boasts Balinese-style cottages and villas set in landscaped gardens. Very personalised service. Other nice touches include villa pools, private courtyards and open-air massage parlours. There are two restaurants, a range of recreational facilities and cultural performances. $$$$

Jimbaran (0361)
This curving white-sand beach between Kuta and Nusa Dua has been developed as another enclave of up-market tourism. Because of its much smaller size and fishing village atmosphere, it has a more intimate feel than sprawling Nusa Dua.

Bali Inter-Continental
Jl Uluwatu, Jimbaran
Tel: 701888; Fax: 701777
An ideal place to view Bali's spectacular sunset, this up-market hotel is set in immense landscaped gardens, with restaurants, pools, spa, tennis courts and watersports facilities. $$$

Four Seasons Resort
Jl Uluwatu, Jimbaran
Tel: 701010; Fax: 701020
Consistently voted one of the top resorts in the world by *Condé Nast Traveler*. Built on a terraced hillside with spectacular views of Jimbaran Bay and Gunung Agung. Set amidst lush landscaped gardens and connected by paths, this resort boasts luxury villas with private splash pools. Extensive spa treatments promise to pamper you beyond belief. $$$$

Ritz-Carlton
Jl Karang Mas Sejahtera, Jimbaran
Tel: 702222; Fax: 701555
High standards of service as expected from this upscale chain of hotels. It has 322 rooms in four-storey resort, club rooms and villas (with private plunge pools), all perched on bluff overlooking the ocean. $$$

Above: Poppies is a restful spot in bustling Kuta

practical information

Sanur (0361)

Also in South Bali, protected by a coral lagoon. Rather sedate and expensive but becoming dense with shops and restaurants. Despite the fact that the beach is skimpy and swimming is impossible at low tide, Sanur maintains its reputation for being romantic and up-market.

Bali Hyatt
Jl Bali Hyatt
Tel: 288271; Fax: 287693
Has been around for over 20 years but kept its age rather well. Set in lush landscaped gardens, which some consider to be Bali's unofficial botanic gardens. Offers luxurious rooms with Balinese decor. There is also a good range of restaurants serving Western, Indonesian, Italian and Chinese cuisine, as well as fresh seafood by the pool. Other amenities include pools, spa and extensive sports facilities, travel centre and shopping arcade. $$$

Hotel Sanur Beach
Jl Danau Tamblingan, Semawang
Tel: 288011; Fax: 287566, 287928
The hotel, with its four-storey block and exclusive bungalows set in landscaped gardens on the beach, is renowned for its friendly staff and excellent service. It offers a range of sports facilities and restaurants which serve Indonesian, Italian, Mexican and South American food. $$

La Taverna Hotel
Jl Danau Tamblingan 29
Tel: 288497; Fax: 287126
Bungalows with cozy verandahs and courtyards are nestled in tropical gardens in this beachfront hotel. A family-friendly place, it also offers child-care services, games and a pool. Its excellent Italian and Indonesian restaurant specialises in oven-fresh pizzas and Balinese *sate*. $$

Taman Agung Beach Inn
Jl Danau Tamblingan 146
Tel: 288549
Very pleasant 35 *losmen*-style rooms with air-conditioning or fan. All have hot water and face a well-kept garden. Minutes from the beach. Laundry, restaurant. $

Nusa Dua / Tanjung Benoa (0361)

Nusa Dua is rather isolated but provides a 'total' hotel environment – everything you could possibly ask for is available on the premises. Restaurants and souvenir shops line the road outside the complex, and the Galleria Nusa Dua shopping complex features restaurants, shops and a supermarket. The downside is that Nusa Dua has precious little personality. Tanjung Benoa point, the northward continuation of Nusa Dua Beach, is lined with more hotels and watersports operations.

Bali Cliff Resort
Pura Batu Pageh, Ungasan
Tel: 771992/3/4, 771364; Fax: 771993
Suites high up a cliff offer unobstructed views of the Indian Ocean from sunrise to sunset. Despite its isolated setting, this self-contained hotel offers five-star facilities: fitness spa, shopping arcade, business centre, theatre, sports and Olympic-size swimming pool. Restaurants offer Italian, Japanese, Continental cuisine, as well as seafood. $$$

Bali Tropik Hotel
34A Jl Pratama, Tanjung Benoa
Tel: 772130, 772107/8/9; Fax: 772131
A three-star resort with an 'all-inclusive' concept; its deluxe rooms and suites are set in peaceful gardens and come with a balcony or terrace. All meals are included in the price, even beverages. Non-motorised watersports like windsurfing and catamaran sailing are also free, as are tennis, billiard and cultural performances. $$

Right: Nusa Dua beach

Grand Hyatt Bali
Nusa Dua
Tel: 771234, 772038; Fax: 772038
Hailed as one of the best resort hotels in Asia, this grand 'water palace' boasts landscaped gardens and carp-filled lagoons, six swimming pools with a 50-m (164-ft) water slide, beautiful beachfront, luxurious suites and bungalows, and a conference theatre. Other facilities include an in-house clinic, fitness centre and a five-hole putting green. $$$

Meliá Bali
Nusa Dua
Tel: 771510; Fax: 771360/2
This luxury resort with a huge lagoon-style pool winding through tropical gardens has rooms, suites and exclusive villas with private plunge pools. It also boasts an extensive range of dining options, variety shows, recreational facilities and a spa. $$$

Nusa Dua Beach Hotel
Nusa Dua
Tel: 771210, 772617/8; Fax: 771229
Spectacular landscaped grounds surround this hotel's luxurious suites and bungalows, with private butler service for guests in the Palace Wing. Expect five-star facilities (pool, spa, gym, squash courts, and so on) whether for children, business travellers or holidaymakers. $$$

Puri Tanjung Hotel Resort
62 Jl Pratama, Tanjung Benoa
Tel: 772121; Fax: 772424
This place offers bungalows and suites with

a beautiful seaside location and a swimming pool. The 24-hour restaurant serves fresh seafood buffets and European food. $$

Ubud (0361)
The Ubud area has a huge number of accommodations to suit all budgets. Ubud encompasses a vast area, from Mas in the south, Andong, Sayan and Payangan in the north, Penestanan in the west and Peliatan in the east. Practically anywhere outside of Ubud town proper – where restaurants and shops abound – will give you more quiet, although food and transport could be a problem.

Amandari
Sayan, Kedewatan
Tel: 975333; Fax: 975335
One of the most romantic hotels in the world, it is set on the very edge of the Ayung river gorge. Its luxurious suites in classical Balinese-style pavilions are connected by winding, landscaped paths. Enjoy a host of facilities and beautiful views of the river valley below. Its restaurant is known for its Western and Indonesian specialities. $$$$

Ananda Cottages
Campuhan, Ubud
Tel: 975376; Fax: 975375
Set amidst rice fields, this lovely property has Balinese-style rooms with fans or air-conditioning. It is close to the Ubud market and is ideal for families. Try *betutu* (smoked duck) at the hotel's Indonesian restaurant. $$

The Chedi
Melinggih Kelod, Payangan
Tel: 975963; Fax: 975968
It boasts spacious bungalows strung out along a ridge with breathtaking views of rice terrace, mountain and river valley. Amenities include two restaurants, a pool, full spa facilities and an art gallery. $$$$

Four Seasons Sayan
Sayan, Ubud
Tel: 977577; Fax: 977588
This peaceful highland retreat boasts luxurious suites and villas (with private plunge pools and outdoor showers) built into an unusual circular structure among rice terraces in the Ayung river valley. $$$$

Above: plush Amandari hotel

Komaneka Resort
Jl Monkey Forest, Ubud
Tel: 976090; Fax: 977140
Charming bungalows with elegant interiors. Set in beautiful gardens in the centre of Ubud but away from the road. Amenities include a restaurant, pool, spa, boutique and art gallery. Romantic and peaceful. $$$

Ulun Ubud
Sanggingan, Ubud
Tel: 975024; Fax: 975524
A gem of a hotel carved into the hillside, this place offers value for money, with spacious cottages, beautiful art on the hotel grounds, and a pool offering stunning views of the ravine and paddy fields. $$

Kintamani / Batur (0366)

Most of the accommodation at Gunung Batur is basic, with cold mountain-spring water and magnificent views. Penelokan has the views, Kintamani is quieter and Toya Bungkah down at the lake gets great sunrises and sunsets.

Jero Wijaya Lakeside Cottages
Toya Bungkah, Songan
Tel: 51249, 51251; Fax: 51250
This group of cottages is set in a quiet location right at the edge of Danau Batur. $$

Lakeview Restaurant & Hotel
Penelokan, Kintamani
Tel: 51394; Tel/Fax: 51464
Perched on the edge of Gunung Batur, this place offers spacious rooms and a good restaurant with a view. $

Candi Dasa / Karangasem (0363)

A small but developed beach resort on the southeast coast between Padangbai and Amlapura (Karangasem), close to the countryside of East Bali. Uncontrolled mining of Candi Dasa's protective coral reef in the 1980s for construction means that the beach is nearly gone. Just 5km (3 miles) from Candi Dasa is the black-sand beaches of Buitan (Balina beach).

Amankila
Manggis, Karangasem
Tel: 41333; Fax: 41555/6
Voted one of the top international resort hideaways by *Condé Naste Traveler*, this luxury complex has a breathtaking cliff-edge setting high above the Lombok Strait, with lots of stairs, dramatic ocean views, fine restaurants and full resort facilities. $$$$

Rama Ocean View Bungalows
Sengkidu, Candi Dasa
Tel: 41974; Fax: 41975
Beachside location away from the main road, with a large pool, tennis court, sauna, and diving and snorkelling facilities. The hotel also has a restaurant and friendly staff. $$

The Watergarden Cottages
Candi Dasa
Tel: 41540; Fax: 41164
A peaceful, romantic hotel with private bungalows set away from the beach. It is noted for its prize-winning tropical gardens, tranquil ambience and friendly staff. Not to be missed is the hotel's TJ's Café. $$

Lovina / Buleleng (0362)

On the north coast, just west of Singaraja. Quiet and unpretentious beach resort area, with black-sand beaches.

Angsoka Cottages
Kalibukbuk, Lovina
Tel: 41268; Fax: 41023
Beautiful garden setting, with a range of rooms, friendly staff and restaurants serving European, Chinese and Indonesian food. $

Banyualit Beach Inn
Kalibukbuk, Lovina
Tel: 41789; Fax: 41563
Attractive rooms and bungalows by the beach; quiet and well managed. The atmosphere is friendly and the restaurant is excellent. Other amenities: money-changer, tour services and watersports. $$

Damai Lovina Villas
Jl Damai, Kayuputih, Lovina
Tel: 41008; Fax: 41009
Only eight luxurious villas set on a mountain slope and surrounded by rice paddies, spice plantations and tropical jungle. A quite and tranquil getaway, with a restaurant manned by a prize-winning chef. $$$

Matahari Beach Resort
Desa Pemuteran, Buleleng
Tel: 92312; Fax: 92313
Luxurious Balinese-style bungalows with garden showers only metres from the beach. Fully-equipped dive centre, restaurant, bar, pool, watersports facilities, and only 30-minute boat ride to Menjangan island. $$$

Mimpi Resort
Banyuwedang, Buleleng
Mobile tel: 0828-362729; Fax: 361088
This luxury beach resort has a thermal spring and diving centre. It can arrange the boat trip and required permit for a snorkelling or diving experience around Menjangan island and is part of West Bali National Park. $$$

Bedugul (0368) / Tabanan (0361)
Bedugul Hotel & Restaurant
Bedugul, Tabanan
Tel: 226593
This comfortable place high up in the mountains has motel-style rooms and bungalows. The restaurant, with a superb lake view, has an a la carte menu as well as buffets. $$

Le Meridien Nirwana Resort
Jl Raya Tanah Lot, Tabanan
Tel: 815900; Fax: 815901
This five-star hotel boasts luxury villas, spa, pools and an 18-hole golf course near a picturesque temple. There's also authentic Asian cuisine like the local *rijstaffel* (rice dish served with a variety of foods), grilled seafood and Italian favourites. $$$$

Pacung Cottages
Pacung, Tabanan
Tel: 225824, 225746
The cottages offer spectacular views of the surrounding rice terraces. There's also a restaurant and a heated pool. $$

Jembrana (0365)
Medewi Beach Cottages
Medewi Beach, Jembrana
Tel: 40029, 40030; Fax: 41555
A pleasant place to relax, with peaceful bungalows and an attractive pool. Standard rooms and a cheap restaurant are on one side of the road, with the more expensive rooms and a classier restaurant on the other. $$

HEALTH & EMERGENCIES
General Health / Pharmacies
Avoid iced drinks and take only bottled water, but be careful of digestive problems from eating too much spicy food. Charcoal tablets and diarrhoea remedies are available in *apotik* (pharmacies) found in every town and city. The sun can be fierce, so protect yourself with sunscreen lotion and a wide-brimmed hat or an umbrella.

Medical / Dental Services
Buy adequate medical insurance before travelling. Serious cases are flown to Singapore, and insurance is required to cover the high cost of chartering a plane and medical team. The local **International SOS** office with 24-hour emergency service is at Jl Bypass Ngurah Rai 24X, Kuta, tel: 755768.

Every regional town centre has a *rumah sakit umum* (public hospital) with varying qualities of services and equipment. The best are **Wangaya** (tel: 222141) and **Kasih Ibu** (tel: 223036) in Denpasar, and in Gianyar (tel: 943049). For minor ailments, go to:
Kuta: **Bali Clinic**, Jl Oberoi 54XX, Kerobokan (tel: 733301); **Kuta Clinic**, Jl Raya Kuta (tel: 753268).
Sanur: **Bali Hyatt Hotel Clinic** (tel: 288271); **Klinik Sanur**, Jl Bypass Ngurah Rai (tel: 289076).
Nusa Dua: **Nusa Dua Clinic**, Jl Pratama 81 (tel: 771324); **Nusa Dua Medical Service**, J Kawasan Wisata (tel: 772118).
Ubud: **Clinic Mas**, Jl Raya Mas, Ubud (tel: 974573); **Ubud Clinic**, Jl Raya Ubud (tel: 974911).

COMMUNICATIONS & POST
Post
The main *kantor pos* (post office) is at Jl Raya Puputan Renon, Denpasar, tel: 223568, open daily 8am–8pm. Service is rather slow and expensive. Major hotels and tourist centres handle basic postal services.

Telecommunications
Coin-operated and card telephones are usually located along noisy roadsides, making

hearing and speaking difficult. Phone cards are available at shops in most towns. Internet cafes are found in most tourist centres.

The main *telkom* office is at Jl Teuku Umar 6, Denpasar, tel: 232111, open 24 hours daily; and nearly every major town and city has one. Many villages have smaller *wartel* (telephone kiosks) with basic services. Other offices in tourist centres are:

Kuta: **Adi Primantara Utama**, Jl Bakung Sari; **Cendana Putih**, Jl Raya Kuta; **Jasa Nusantara**, Jl Seminyak.

Sanur: **Anggar Ari Agung**, Jl Danau Tamblingan 174; **Danghyang Nirarta**, Jl Cemara 9X.

Nusa Dua: **Dharmajaya**, Jl Bypass Ngurah Rai.

Bali area codes: (0361) Denpasar, Gianyar, Kuta, Nusa Dua, Sanur, Tabanan; (0362) Singaraja; (0363) Amlapura; (0365) Negara; (0366) Bangli, Klungkung; (0368) Bedugul. Indonesia's country code is (62).

Useful Numbers
Ambulance: 118
Directory Assistance: 108
Immigration: 227828, 751038
Information: 162
International Operator: 101
Police: 110
Red Cross: 225465

USEFUL INFORMATION

Dance Performances
Barong & Rangda: Batubulan (daily 9.30am); Kesiman, Denpasar (daily 9.30am); Mawang, Batuan (Thur, Sat 7pm); Padangtegal Kelod, Ubud (Mon 7pm); Peliatan (Wed 7pm); Puri Saren Ubud (Fri 7pm); Suwung, Denpasar (daily 9am).
Kecak: Padangtegal Kaja, Ubud (Sat, Sun, Wed 7pm); Bona (Sun, Mon, Wed, Fri 7pm); Padangtegal Kelod, Ubud (Tues 7.30pm); Puri Agung Peliatan (Thur 7.30pm); Pura Dalem Puri, Ubud (Fri 7.30pm); Junjungan (Mon 7pm); Waribang, Denpasar (daily 6.30pm).
Sanghyang Dedari and **Sanghyang Jaran**: See Ubud, Bona and Padangtegal under *Kecak*.

Right: young festival participant

Gambuh: 1st and 15th of every month, Pura Desa, Batuan (7pm).
Sendratari: Ubud (Sun, Wed 7.30pm) and Teges, Peliatan (Tues 7.30pm).
Tari Kodok: Sanur Beach Hotel (Sun 7pm).
Gebyug: Pura Dalem Puri Ubud (Mon 7.30pm).
Tari Lepas: Puri Saren Ubud (Mon, Wed, Sat 7.30pm); Peliatan (Sun, Fri 7.30pm); at restaurants in Nusa Dua, Sanur and Kuta (see *Eating Out, pages 75–9*).
Wayang Kulit: Oka Kartini Hotel, Ubud (Sun, Wed 8pm).

Spas / Massage
Soothe your muscles, relieve stress or pamper yourself with a variety of massage techniques. Many resort hotels offer spa facilities (see *Accommodation, pages 91–6*), but other recommended independent places are:
Kuta: **Spa at The Villas**, Jl Kunti 118X, Seminyak, Kuta, tel: 730840.
Ubud: **Bodywork**, Jl Hanuman 25, Padangtegal, Ubud, tel: 975720; **Nur**, Jl Hanoman 28, Padangtegal, Ubud, tel: 975352; **Ubud Sari**, Jl Kajeng 35, Ubud, tel: 974393.
Sanur: **Peruna**, Jl Danau Tamblingan 162, Sanur, tel: 289536.

Golf
Bali Golf & Country Club: 18-hole course near the coast, one of Asia's best five. Nusa Dua, tel: 771791.
Bali Handara Kosaido Country Club: 18-hole course rated in the world's top 25, located high in the mountains. Bedugul, tel: (0362) 22182; (0361) 289431.
Grand Bali Beach: Challenging 9-hole course. Sanur, tel: 288511.

Nirwana Bali Golf Club: Picturesque 18-hole course among coastal rice paddies near Pura Tanah Lot. Tabanan, tel: 815960.

Diving / Watersports
Bali is a good place to learn to dive, although the quality of the dive sites is not the best that you can find in Indonesia. The following operations specialise in dive packages and courses, some of which also offer a range of watersports.
Kuta: **Prodive**, Kuta Centre Block F14-15, tel: 753951; **Baruna Water Sport**, Jl Bypass Ngurah Rai, Kuta, tel: 753820.
Sanur: **Ena Dive Centre**, Jl Tirta Ening 1, Sanur, tel: 288829; **Kesuma Sari Beach Club**, Jl Kesuma Sari 19, Sanur, tel: 289803.
Nusa Dua: **Taman Sari Marine Sports**, Tanjung Benoa, Nusa Dua, tel: 772583; **Yos Diving**, Jl Pratima, Nusa Dua, tel: 773774.
Singaraja: **Spice Dive**, Jl Raya Seririt, Singaraja, tel: (0362) 41305.

Cruises
Bali Hai: Luxury catamaran to Nusa Lembongan and for sunset dinner cruises. Benoa Harbour, tel: 720331.
Mabua Express: For quick service to Nusa Lembongan. Benoa Harbour, tel: 772521.
Ombak Putih: Sail in comfort on a traditional Buginese schooner. Jl Tirta Empul 14, Sanur, tel: 287934.
Sea Safari Cruises: A wide choice of cruises. Jl Raya Sesetan, Denpasar, tel: 721495.
Wakalouka Cruises: Luxury catamaran trip to Nusa Lembongan and Wakanusa Resort. Jl Padang Kartika 5X, Denpasar, tel: 426972.

Trekking / Rafting / Kayaking
The best rafting is during the rainy season from November to March. Some of the following operators also organise kayaking, trekking and mountain-biking trips:
Bali Adventure Rafting, Jl Diponegoro 150 B-29, Denpasar, tel: 238759.
Bali Safari Rafting, Jl Raya Puputan 6, Denpasar, tel: 221315.
Jero Wijaya Tourist Service, Jl Raya Andong, Petulu, Ubud, tel: 973172.
Sobek, Jl Tirta Ening 9, Sanur, tel: 287059.

Surfing
Kuta was famous for surfing, but there are better locations at Suluban, Canggu and Medewi. Surfing is reasonably good all year, especially from June to August.

Equipment can be rented at most beaches, or bought in Kuta at **Dream Land Surf Shop**, Kuta Square Block D-24 (tel: 755159); **MCD Shop**, Jl Nyangnyang Sari 17 (tel: 735155) and Jl Legian (tel: 754583); **Quiksilver**, Jl Raya Kuta 69X (tel: 751214); **Surfer Girl**, Jl Legian 318 (tel: 752693).

USEFUL ADDRESSES

Tourist Offices
Bali Tourist Information Centre, Jl Bunisari 7, Kuta, tel: 754090.
Badung Tourist Office, Jl S Parman, Niti Mandala, Renon, Denpasar, tel: 222387.
Bina Wisata Ubud Tourist Office, Ubud main crossroad, tel: 973285.
Buleleng Tourist Office, Jl Veteran 23, Singaraja, tel: (0362) 25141.
Jembrana Tourist Office, Jl Dr Setia Budi 1, Negara, tel: (0365) 41060.

Online Services
Check out these websites:
www.bali-paradise.com
www.indo.com
www.goarchi.com/oc

Airline Offices
Ansett Australia, Grand Bali Beach, Sanur, tel: 289636.
Air France, Grand Bali Beach, Sanur, tel: 287734.
Cathay Pacific, Grand Bali Beach, Sanur, tel: 286001.
China Airlines, Ngurah Rai Airport, tel: 754856.

Left: a helping hand

Continental, Grand Bali Beach, Sanur, tel: 287774.
Eva Air, Ngurah Rai Airport, Tuban, tel: 751011 ext. 1638, fax: 756488.
Garuda Indonesia, Grand Bali Beach, Sanur, tel: 288243. Natour Kuta Beach, tel: 751179. Nusa Dua, tel: 771864, 771444.
Japan Airlines, Grand Bali Beach, Sanur, tel: 287576/7.
Lauda Air, Jl Bypass Ngurah Rai 12, Kuta, tel: 758686.
Malaysian Airlines, Grand Bali Beach, Sanur, tel: 285071/2/3. Ngurah Rai Airport, tel: 756132.
Merpati Nusantara, Jl Melati 51, Denpasar, tel: 235358.
Qantas, Grand Bali Beach, Sanur, tel: 288331/2/3. Ngurah Rai Airport, tel: 288823/4. Kertha Wijaya Shopping Centre, Denpasar, tel: 237343.
Singapore Airlines, Bank Bali Building, Jl Dewi Sartika 88, Denpasar, tel: 261666.
Thai Airways, Ngurah Rai Airport, Sanur, tel: 754856.

Consulates

Australia (also represents **Canada**, **New Zealand & United Kingdom**), Jl Prof Moh Yamin 4, Renon, Denpasar, tel: 235092, fax: 231990.
Finland & Sweden, Segara Village Hotel, Jl Segara Ayu, Sanur, tel: 288407/8, fax: 288021.
France, Smailing Tours, Jl Bypass Ngurah Rai 88X, Sanur, tel/fax: 288224.
Germany, Jl Pantai Karang 17, Sanur, tel: 288535, fax: 288826.
Italy, Lotus Enterprise Building, Jl Bypass Ngurah Rai, Jimbaran, tel/fax: 701005.
Japan, Jl Raya Puputan, Renon, Denpasar, tel: 234808, fax: 231308.
Netherlands, KCB Travel, Jl Raya Kuta 127, Kuta, tel: 751517, fax: 752777.
Norway & Denmark, Jl Jayagiri VIII/10, Denpasar, tel: 235098, fax: 234834.
Spain, Melia Hotel, Nusa Dua, tel: 711510, ext 88078.
Switzerland & Austria, Swiss Restaurant, Jl Pura Bagus Teruna, Legian Kaja, tel: 751735, fax: 754457.
United States, Jl Hayam Wuruk 188, Denpasar, tel: 223605, fax: 222426.

FURTHER READING

General
The Island of Bali by Miguel Covarrubias. Periplus, Singapore, 1999.
Insight Guide: *Bali*. Apa Publications, Singapore, 2000.
Bali: The Ultimate Island by Leonard Lueras. Times, Singapore, 1987.
The Balinese by Hugh Mabbett. January Books, Wellington, 1988.

History
A Tale from Bali by Vicki Baum. Periplus, Singapore, 1999.
Bali: A Paradise Created by Adrian Vickers. Periplus, Singapore, 1989.
Monumental Bali by A J Bernet Kempers and Van Goor Zonen. Periplus, Singapore, 1991.
Visible and Invisible Realms by Margaret J Wiener. University of Chicago Press, 1995.

Religion / Culture
Trance in Bali by Jane Belo. Columbia University Press, New York, 1960.
Offerings by Francine Brinkgreve and David Stuart-Fox. Image Network Indonesia, Sanur, 1992.

Art / Music / Dance
The Art and Culture of Bali by Urs Ramseyer. Oxford in Asia, Singapore, 1977.
Music in Bali by Colin McPhee. Yale University Press, 1966.
Balinese Music by Michael Tenzer. Periplus, Singapore, 1992.
Dance and Drama in Bali by Beryl de Zoete and Walter Spies. Oxford, Singapore, 1973.
Balinese Paintings (second edition) by A A M Djelantik. Oxford in Asia, Singapore, 1990.
The Development of Painting in Bali (second edition) by Suteja Neka and Garrett Kam. Yayasan Dharma Seni, Ubud, 1998.
Perceptions of Paradise by Garrett Kam. Yayasan Dharma Seni, Ubud, 1993.
Walter Spies and Balinese Art by Hans Rhodins and John Darling. Zutphen Terra, Amsterdam, 1980.
Textiles in Bali by Brigitta Hauser-Schaublin, et al. Periplus, Singapore, 1991.

INSIGHT
Pocket Guides

Insight Pocket Guides pioneered a new approach to guidebooks, introducing the concept of the authors as "local hosts" who would provide readers with personal recommendations, just as they would give honest advice to a friend who came to stay. They also included a full-size pull-out map. Now, to cope with the needs of the 21st century, new editions in this growing series are being given a new look to make them more practical to use, and restaurant and hotel listings have been greatly expanded.

INSIGHT GUIDES

The world's largest collection of visual travel guides

Now in association with

ACKNOWLEDGEMENTS

Cover	**Patrick Ward/Colorific**
Backcover	**G.P. Reichelt**
Photography	**Jack Hollingsworth and**
Pages 42	**Heather Angel**
12, 35, 36, 72	**Hans Höfer**
20	**J. Houyvet/HBL**
2/3, 8/9, 23, 26T, 29, 39, 40, 53B,	
55T, 63, 71, 76, 79, 83, 92, 98	**Ingo Jezierski**
25B	**Robert Knight**
47, 49T	**G.P. Reichelt**
11	**University at Leiden, Amsterdam**
Cartography	**Michael Larby**
Cover Design	**Carlotta Junger**
Production	**Tanvir Virdee/Caroline Low**

INDEX